★ HOMEMADE ★
TAKEAWAYS

ROB ALLISON

HOMEMADE TAKEAWAYS

How to make your favourite takeaway... but better

100 RECIPES

ROB ALLISON

First published in Great Britain in 2015
by Orion Publishing Group Ltd
Carmelite House, 50 Victoria Embankment
London EC4Y 0DZ
An Hachette UK Company

10 9 8 7 6 5 4 3 2 1

A CIP catalogue record for this book
is available from the British Library.

ISBN: 9781409154631

Photography by Kris Kirkham
Design by Smith & Gilmour
Home economist: Leonie Sookie
Prop stylist: Jenny Iggledon
Copy-edited by Imogen Fortes
Project-edited by Kate Wanwimolruk
Proofread by Jenny Wheatley
Indexed by Elizabeth Wiggans

Printed and bound in China

The Orion Publishing Group's policy is to use papers that
are natural, renewable and recyclable products and made
from wood grown in sustainable forests. The logging and
manufacturing processes are expected to conform to the
environmental regulations of the country of origin.

www.orionbooks.co.uk

by BOOK or by COOK
COOKING
EATING
SHARING

For lots more delicious recipes plus articles,
interviews and videos from the best chefs
cooking today visit our blog
bybookorbycook.co.uk

Follow us
 @bybookorbycook

Find us
 facebook.com/bybookorbycook

MENU

INTRODUCTION

Takeaway food is comfort food. It is comforting because you don't have to cook, it is comforting because you don't have to wash up, and it is comforting because it can be enjoyed within the confines of your own home sitting on your sofa. It is a wonder of the age we live in that almost any culinary craving can be sated by a short phone call and scooter driver.

The neon lights of the takeaway twinkle above almost every high street, and the delicious aromas of grilling meat and bubbling spices tempt you to forget about cooking at home and to order something over the counter instead. Curries, sushi, burgers and kebabs (to name just a few) are all instantly available and have become very much part of our modern gastro-psyche. But here lies the problem with takeaway food: we are so accustomed to its presence that we take it for granted. It is no longer seen as food to be occasionally eaten as a treat; instead too many now consider takeaway food to be an acceptable substitute for home-cooked meals.

The great dishes that collectively make up some of our favourite takeaways – from fish 'n' chips to chicken tikka masala – have gradually moved away from their original incarnations. Instead vibrantly flavoured treats have become ugly imitations that are carelessly slopped out to the masses. The worst purveyors of takeaway food have realised that by adding extra fats, sugars and chemicals to substandard ingredients they can increase their profit margins and their speed of service.

This book is my attempt to reclaim some of our favourite takeaway dishes back into the home. I think we need to remind ourselves that the food we love to eat has a history and an origin; that there was a time when it was prepared with attention and thought – that is what made it so popular in the first place. Takeaway food doesn't have to be eaten with a guilty conscience; it doesn't have to be ordered over the phone and gobbled down in a mad frenzy in front of the television. When cooked at home, classics such as chicken korma are transformed from a bland sauce bobbing with overcooked chicken into a resplendent meal bursting with satisfying flavours and textures that any cook should be proud of placing in front of their family. By comparing your fresh korma to the tepid gloop that is so often delivered you will see that the point of this book is to highlight the difference between real cooking and the lazy offerings of the bad takeaway.

This is by no means a health or diet book, but by simply being able to control the quality of ingredients you use to prepare these recipes you will naturally cook infinitely healthier and tastier food than you will find in most takeaways. While some recipes are very quick to prepare and will be ready in less time than it takes the delivery boy or girl to ring your doorbell, we must all realise that sometimes cooking takes a little longer. Some dishes will need time to marinate and cook. However, I guarantee that you will reap the rewards of your patience – not only will your food taste better, it won't leave you reaching for antacids in the middle of the night. This book will also undoubtedly save you money. Even if you only ever replace one of your takeaway meals for four with a recipe from the book you will have economised.

I can assure you that by substituting those 40 minutes of delivery waiting time sitting in monotonous silence in front of the telly with 40 minutes of preparation and cooking, you may learn to enjoy cooking and see it as a means to transition between work, family and home. There are few greater joys in life than cooking for those you love, and knowing that you have done the best for them. Don't miss out on this feeling because you can't be bothered. Use your love of the takeaway to take you back into the kitchen. Cook from this book and experience how good takeaway food can taste.

NOTES FOR COOKS

★ All eggs are medium unless otherwise stated.

★ All fruit and vegetables are medium-sized unless otherwise stated.

★ Vegetables such as onions, garlic and carrots are assumed to be peeled unless otherwise stated.

★ To sterilise jars, preheat your oven to 130°C/ fan 120°C/250°F/gas mark ½. Throughly wash your jars in the hottest soapy water your gloved hands can handle before rinsing under hot running water. Place the jars into the hot oven to dry.

CHAPTER ✳
ONE
→ # INDIAN

Due to the size of India and the international influences it has been touched by over the years, there are few other countries in the world that include so many ingredients in their cuisine. Don't let this put you off though, as buying just a small number of select spices and cooking them with onions, garlic and ginger is enough to produce a fantastic homemade curry to rival any takeaway offering.

Certainly Indian takeaways can serve up tasty curries, but all too often the ingredients they use are substandard and the meat, fish or vegetables end up drowning in a pool of excess oil. Indian food cooked at home will feel lighter – still satisfyingly deep in flavour, but without the acrid after-taste of old oil and overly fatty meats. It is also worth noting that most curries taste best the day after they have been cooked and have had time for the flavours and spices to blend and mellow.

ONION BHAJIA

MAKES 12 – SERVES 4

Bhajia should be deliciously crisp, deeply flavoured balls of joy, not the dark brown, flaccid specimens that are so often cooked up and dropped off by the local takeaway driver. Prepared at home, and served fresh from the fryer whilst still hot and delicious, these Bhajia are streets ahead of any takeaway temptation.

PREP TIME: 15 MINS
COOKING TIME: 10 MINS

1 onion, finely sliced
1 red onion, finely sliced
75g gram (chickpea) flour
75g cornflour
1 green chilli, finely chopped
    (seeds removed if you
    don't like it too hot)
1 tsp nigella (black onion)
    seeds
2 tsp ground turmeric
1 tsp Kashmiri chilli powder
    (or cayenne pepper)
1 small potato, grated
about 1 litre sunflower
    or vegetable oil, for
    deep-frying
salt
Quick Mango Chutney
    (see page 14), to serve
lemon wedges, to serve
    (optional)
coriander leaves, to serve
    (optional)

Place both types of onion along with both the flours in a bowl. Add the green chilli, nigella seeds, turmeric, chilli powder and potato. Pour in 50ml water and mix well with a wooden spoon. Slowly add about 50ml more water, continuing to stir, until you have a thick batter that clings to all of the other ingredients.

In a large high-sided saucepan, heat about 15cm of oil until it reaches 180°C. It really is advisable to buy a temperature probe for deep-frying, but if you don't have one, drop a little of the batter into the oil when you think it is ready. The oil is at the correct temperature if the batter bubbles and floats to the surface, turning golden brown in about 30 seconds.

When ready to fry, take a large serving spoon and dip it briefly in the hot oil. Dig the slicked spoon into the batter and heap large mounds (as close to a twelfth of the mixture as possible) straight into the hot oil. Do not overcrowd your pan at this point; each ball should have space enough to bob around to ensure crispy bhajia. Fry the bhajia for 3–4 minutes, by which time they should be lightly golden all over. When cooked, remove to kitchen paper to drain any excess fat.

Sprinkle your bhajia with a little salt before serving with the mango chutney, lemon wedges and a scattering of coriander leaves, if using.

CURRIED CAULIFLOWER, PEAS and PANEER

SERVES 4–6

There is something about the flavour of cauliflower that lends itself so well to heavy spices. I can't quite put my finger on it, but a bit like beetroot, cauliflower has a sweet earthiness that is capable of carrying robust flavours. Use the spices and the cooking method of this dish as a template for other vegetables; boiled potatoes work brilliantly, as do courgettes.

PREP TIME: 15 MINS
COOKING TIME: 12 MINS

1 head of cauliflower,
    florets only
3 tbsp vegetable or
    sunflower oil
1 tbsp yellow mustard seeds
24 curry leaves
2 tbsp garam masala
about 2 tsp chilli powder
    – more or less as
    you prefer
200g paneer, roughly diced
    into 1cm cubes
100g frozen peas
5 spring onions, trimmed
    and thinly sliced
juice of 1 lemon
2 red chillies, deseeded
    and finely diced

Bring a large pot of water to the boil. Add a generous amount of salt, then drop in the prepared cauliflower florets. Simmer the florets for 4 minutes, before draining through a colander and immediately running under cold water until completely cool. Leave the cauliflower to drain.

Heat the oil in a large frying pan over a medium-high heat. When hot add the mustard seeds and curry leaves. Fry for about 45 seconds; the mustard seeds will begin to pop and the curry leaves will shrivel a little.

Add the garam masala and chilli powder and continue to fry, stirring continuously for 20 seconds. Increase the heat to maximum and add the cooked cauliflower and the paneer. Fry, stirring regularly for 2–3 minutes, before adding the frozen peas and spring onions. Continue to fry for a further minute, by which time the peas should be just cooked through.

Remove the pan from the heat, add the lemon juice and toss through the red chilli. Serve immediately.

QUICK MANGO CHUTNEY

MAKES ENOUGH TO FILL 2 X 350ML JARS

Spicey, sweet and sour all work in harmony in this chutney which sits as comfortably with cold ham as it does with the Onion Bhajia on page 10. Needless to say, if you like things a little more spicy then just leave the seeds in the red chillies.

PREP TIME: 15 MINS
COOKING TIME: 10 MINS

2 tbsp sultanas
1 tsp cumin seeds
1 cinnamon stick,
    snapped in half
75g caster sugar
75ml red wine vinegar
2 red chillies, deseeded
    and finely chopped
2cm piece fresh ginger,
    peeled and grated
4 mangoes, peeled,
    stoned and chopped
    into 1cm slices

Place the sultanas in a bowl and pour over enough boiling water to cover. Leave to plump up whilst you continue with the rest of the recipe.

Heat a medium saucepan over a medium-high heat and tip in the cumin seeds and cinnamon stick. Dry-fry the spices for 25 seconds or until they turn a shade browner and release their delicious scent. Remove the pan from the heat and pour in both the sugar and the vinegar. Stir the ingredients off the heat a little so the sugar begins to dissolve into the vinegar. Place the pan back on the heat and bring to the vinegar to the boil, stirring regularly to dissolve the sugar.

Drain the sultanas and add along with the remaining ingredients. Simmer for about 8 minutes, by which time the mango should just be starting to break down and the chutney will have thickened.

Serve immediately or cool to room temperature. This chutney can last up to a week if kept in an airtight container in the fridge.

TOMATO and TAMARIND RELISH

MAKES ENOUGH TO FILL 2 X 350ML JARS

This is a lightly spiced relish that is best served cold.
If ever you find yourself with a glut of old tomatoes then this
is the recipe to turn to as the riper the tomato the better.

PREP TIME: 15 MINS
COOKING TIME: 25 MINS

2 tbsp sunflower or
    vegetable oil
1 tsp brown mustard seeds
1 green chilli, finely chopped
    (remove the seeds if you
    don't like heat)
1 small red onion,
    finely chopped
3cm piece fresh ginger,
    grated
2 cloves garlic, finely
    chopped
5 ripe tomatoes, roughly
    chopped into 2cm chunks
1 heaped tbsp tamarind
    pulp, mixed with 150ml
    warm water
2 tbsp desiccated coconut
3 tsp red wine vinegar

Heat the oil in a medium saucepan over a medium-high heat. When hot add the mustard seeds and heat until they begin to pop. At this point tip in the chilli, onion, ginger and garlic. Fry, stirring regularly for 3–4 minutes, by which time the onions should have softened.

Add the tomatoes and stir to combine with the rest of the ingredients. Continue frying for a further minute or until the tomatoes just begin to collapse at the edges. Pour in the tamarind mixture and stir.

Bring the mixture to the boil, before reducing the heat to a simmer. Cook like this for about 10 minutes by which time the tomatoes should have collapsed and the mixture will be quite loose. Loosely crush any large pieces of tomato with the back of a fork, then add the coconut and red wine vinegar.

Bring the mixture back to the boil and simmer for a further 5 minutes, by which time the relish should have thickened. Leave to cool before serving.

Once cooked and cooled this relish can be kept covered in the fridge for 5 days.

PRAWN CURRY

SERVES 4

This curry has its roots in the famous fish curries of Goa, an area abundant with fresh seafood and a lighter cooking style to suit. I have also taken a little hint from Thai curries and used a large amount of coriander and splashes of lime juice. If you can't get hold of decent prawns then firm white fish such as cod or pollock work equally well.

PREP TIME: 25 MINS
COOKING TIME: 40 MINS

3 tbsp vegetable or
    sunflower oil
1 large onion, finely diced
1 large bunch of coriander
5 cloves garlic,
    roughly chopped
4cm piece fresh ginger,
    peeled and grated
1 x 400ml tin coconut milk
1 green chilli,
    roughly chopped
1 tsp paprika
1 tbsp ground coriander
2 tsp ground cumin
1 tsp ground turmeric
2 star anise
20 raw king prawns, shelled
    apart from the tail
2 limes
salt and freshly ground
    black pepper

Pour the oil into a large saucepan and warm over a medium heat. When hot add the onion, and fry, stirring regularly for about 10 minutes, by which time the onion should have cooked through and taken on a little colour.

Whilst the onion is cooking place all of the remaining ingredients apart from the star anise, prawns and limes into a food processor along with a generous pinch of salt and pepper. Blitz the ingredients until they create a thick, smooth paste. Keep this to one side.

Add the star anise to the onion and continue to fry for a further 2 minutes. Increase the heat to maximum and when the onion begins to sizzle, add the coriander paste to the saucepan. Bring the whole lot to the boil before reducing the heat to a simmer. Cook the paste like this, stirring regularly for about 15 minutes, by which time the liquid should have reduced by about half and will have a thick consistency.

Whilst the curry is simmering place the prawns in a bowl and season with a little salt. Pour the juice of 1 of the limes over the prawns and leave to sit for 5 minutes.

When the curry sauce has had its 15 minutes tip in the marinated prawns and bring the liquid to the boil. Simmer the curry for 2 minutes, or until the prawns are pink, opaque and cooked through. Squeeze over the second lime and serve.

FISH TIKKA

SERVES 4

The succulent flesh and natural sweetness of fresh fish perfectly complement the intricacies of curry spices. The key is to buy firm white-fleshed fish and to cook it over a high heat. Cod and monkfish are great choices, but if you don't have the budget for these, then fish such as coley and tilapia work just as well.

PREP TIME: 15 MINS,
PLUS MARINATING TIME
COOKING TIME: 10 MINS

8 sea bass fillets (about
    175g each), skinned
    and pin-boned
juice of 1 lemon
2 tsp fine salt
2 tsp ground cumin
250g natural yoghurt
4 cloves garlic, crushed
3cm piece fresh ginger,
    peeled and grated
50g gram (chickpea) flour
1 tbsp garam masala
2 tsp ground coriander
1 tsp smoked paprika
1 tsp ground fenugreek
1 tsp ground turmeric
1 tbsp tomato purée
salt and freshly ground
    black pepper
freshly cooked plain rice,
    to serve
lemon wedges, to serve

Place the fish in a shallow dish and pour over the lemon juice. Massage the juice into the fish before pouring off any excess. Mix the fine salt and cumin, then sprinkle over the fish, again massaging it in to ensure reasonably even coverage. Leave to one side.

Place all the remaining ingredients, except the rice and lemon, into a bowl along with a generous pinch of salt and pepper. Use a wooden spoon to mix until you achieve a smooth paste.

Smooth the marinade all over the fish. Cover and leave to marinate in the fridge for a minimum of 4 hours but preferably overnight.

When ready to cook, heat your grill to maximum. Line your grill tray with foil, then lay a piece of baking parchment on top of the foil. Place the fish on to the baking parchment then slide the tray under the grill, as close as it can be to the hot element. Grill for 6–8 minutes by which time the tikka coating will have browned lightly and a satisfying crust will have developed.

Remove and let the fish sit for 2 minutes before serving with rice and lemon wedges.

CRISPY FRIED SHALLOTS

SERVES 6 AS A GARNISH

These shallots are the perfect finishing touch to almost any curry.
Packing in a deeply delicious savoury flavour and a satisfyingly crunchy
texture, condiments like this will elevate your food and keep you from
reaching for the takeaway menu.

PREP TIME: 5 MINS
COOKING TIME: 10 MINS

**about 500ml vegetable
or sunflower oil for
deep-frying**
**3 banana shallots, finely
sliced lengthways**
Salt

Heat about 5cm of oil in a wide frying pan or saucepan
until it reaches 180°C. You can check the oil is the correct
temperature by dropping in a piece of sliced shallot – it should
bubble and float almost instantly, but not turn brown or
blacken quickly. The best method is to buy a temperature
probe or jam thermometer.

When you are happy with the temperature of the oil, drop in
half the shallots. It is best to cook them in two or more batches
to ensure the oil temperature doesn't drop too much, which
results in soggy shallots.

Fry the shallots for 5–6 minutes, by which time they should
have turned dark golden brown. When ready, use a slotted
spoon to remove the cooked shallots to a clean piece of kitchen
paper to drain any excess oil and season with salt. Repeat the
process with the remaining shallots.

The cooked onions are best cooled and kept in an airtight
container lined with a little kitchen paper. Stored like this
in a cool place they will last at least 3–4 days.

PILAF RICE

SERVES 6

Cooking rice seems to intimidate some people, but it really isn't the impossible task many make it out to be. For this recipe you need an ovenproof pan or dish, but if you don't have one then start your rice on the hob before transferring it to a roasting tray and covering with parchment paper and tin foil. I have chosen to garnish the rice with Crispy Fried Shallots, pomegranate seeds and mint, but treat this recipe as a base to try other flavour combinations.

PREP TIME: 15 MINS
COOKING TIME: 20 MINS

350g basmati rice
1 tbsp sunflower
   or vegetable oil
knob of butter
1 onion, diced
8 cloves
6 cardamom pods,
   lightly crushed with
   the side of a knife
2 bay leaves
2 cinnamon sticks
700ml hot chicken
   or vegetable stock
salt and freshly ground
   black pepper
seeds of 1 pomegranate,
   to serve
1 small bunch of mint
   leaves, to serve
Crispy Fried Shallots
   (see page 20), to serve

Preheat your oven to 180°C/170°C fan/350°F/gas mark 4.

Place the rice in a sieve and run it under cold water for about a minute. Use your fingers to work the water all around the rice. When you have finished rinsing the rice place it in a bowl and cover it with cold water.

Make a cartouche by cutting a circle of baking parchment just a little bigger than the diameter of your pan. Scrunch the paper up and open it up again to make it more pliable.

Heat the oil and butter in an ovenproof pan over a medium-high heat. Once the butter has melted into the oil and is bubbling, add the onion and a good pinch of salt. Fry, stirring regularly for 5 minutes, by which time the onions should have coloured lightly and softened. Add the cloves, cardamom, bay leaves and cinnamon sticks to the pan and continue to stir and fry for a further 2 minutes.

Drain the rice through a sieve, then pour it into the saucepan. Stir the rice around so that it becomes slicked with the flavoured oil. Add a little salt and pepper before pouring in the hot stock. Let the stock come to the boil, place your cartouche on top of the liquid, and slide the saucepan straight into the oven.

Bake the rice for 15 minutes before removing it, and then let it sit for a further 5 minutes. Remove the cartouche, fluff the rice up with a fork and garnish with the pomegranate seeds, mint leaves and crispy shallots.

CHICKEN TIKKA MASALA

SERVES 6

Tikka masala is a ubiquitous dish, so much so that nobody is quite sure where the concept and recipe originated. Whether it was India or Britain, there's no denying that it is delicious curry.

PREP TIME: 25 MINS, PLUS MARINATING TIME
COOKING TIME: 40 MINS

250g natural yoghurt
3 tbsp garam masala
2 tbsp ground coriander
2 tbsp ground ginger
1 tbsp ground cumin
2 tsp smoked paprika
6 cloves garlic, crushed
  to a paste
5cm piece fresh ginger,
  peeled and grated
6 chicken breasts, chopped
  into 4cm pieces
4 tbsp sunflower or
  vegetable oil
2 onions, peeled and puréed
  in a food processor;
  grated if you don't own
  a food processor
6 cloves
2 heaped tbsp tomato purée
1 x 400g tin chopped
  tomatoes
100ml double cream
salt and freshly ground
  black pepper
about 75g flaked almonds,
  toasted, to serve
1 small bunch of chopped
  coriander, to serve

Place half the yoghurt in a large bowl along with half the ground spices and half the garlic and ginger. Add a generous pinch of salt and pepper. Mix well with a spoon until you reach a smooth consistency.

Add the chicken pieces to the marinade, coating them well, then cover and leave in the fridge to marinate for a minimum of 4 hours but preferably overnight.

When ready to cook, heat the oil in a large saucepan over a medium heat. Add the puréed onions to the oil along with a large pinch of salt. Leave to cook, stirring regularly for 12–15 minutes, by which time the onions should have taken on some colour and have become very soft. Add the cloves and the remaining ground spices, garlic and ginger. Continue to fry for a further 2 minutes, stirring almost constantly.

Add the tomato purée and cook for a further 2 minutes, stirring constantly. Increase the heat and add the tinned tomatoes and marinated chicken. Stir all the ingredients whilst you bring them to the boil. Reduce the heat and simmer for 10–12 minutes, until the chicken is fully cooked through. If you're not sure, pick out the thickest piece and cut it open to check. It's cooked when the flesh is white throughout.

Stir in the double cream for a little luxury before serving topped with the toasted almonds and chopped coriander.

PORK DHANSAK

SERVES 4

When I was first introduced to this curry it came loaded with large chunks of pineapple and red pepper. It was delicious and different to many of the other curries in my local takeaway but since my first dhansak I have come to realise that the classic version is cooked with a thick sweet and sour sauce made with lentils, and is unlike that first incarnation I tried. I have gone with my stomach on this one, meaning the following recipe is based on that first delicious, zingy curry I ate many years ago.

PREP TIME: 25 MINS
COOKING TIME: 2 HOURS

3 tbsp vegetable or
    sunflower oil
2 red onions, finely diced
2 cinnamon sticks
6 green cardamom pods,
    lightly crushed with
    the side of a knife
10 cloves
4 cloves garlic, finely diced
4cm piece fresh ginger,
    peeled and grated
2 red chillies, finely diced
    (seeds removed if you
    don't like too much heat)
1 tbsp ground turmeric
1 tbsp ground coriander
1 tbsp ground ginger
1.25kg pork shoulder,
    cut into 4cm chunks
4 tomatoes, roughly chopped
5 tbsp red wine vinegar
½ pineapple (about 300g),
    peeled, core removed, flesh
    chopped into 4cm chunks
    (if you can't source a fresh
    pineapple use drained,
    tinned pineapple)
salted peanuts, roughly
    chopped, to serve (optional)

Heat the oil in a large saucepan over a medium-high heat. When hot add the onions and fry, stirring regularly, for 5–6 minutes, until the onions have softened. Add the cinnamon, cardamom pods and cloves. Continue to fry and stir for a further 2 minutes.

Add the garlic, ginger and red chilli and fry for another minute before adding the ground spices. Fry and stir continuously for a further minute.

Increase the heat to maximum and add the pork shoulder to the pan. Fry, stirring regularly for 2 minutes, by which time the meat should be well coated in the spice mixture. Add the tomatoes, 3 tablespoons of the vinegar and 500ml water, and stir with a wooden spoon, scraping the base of the pan to release any dark meaty sediment that may have stuck to the base. Bring the liquid to the boil, and then reduce the heat to a simmer. Simmer for 1½ hours, topping up the pan with water every now and then so that it doesn't cook dry. After this time the pork should be meltingly soft and the sauce should have thickened.

Add the pineapple, along with the remaining red wine vinegar, and continue cooking for a further 10 minutes. Just before serving scatter the curry with the chopped peanuts, if using.

LAMB SAAG

SERVES 6

Lamb neck is an excellent choice for curry as it contains a decent amount of fat, which when slowly cooked becomes deliciously tender. Chunks of lamb shoulder or leg would work well in this recipe too, as would beef shin if you are looking for a different flavour. To make this even easier, the cashew nut cream at the end can be omitted, but try it because it raises the dish above and beyond the best any Indian takeaway can muster.

PREP TIME: 25 MINS
COOKING TIME: 2 HOURS

3 tbsp garam masala
1 tbsp Kashmiri
    chilli powder
    (or cayenne pepper)
1 tbsp ground turmeric
1.5kg lamb neck,
    chopped into 4cm dice
5 tbsp vegetable or
    sunflower oil
3 onions, peeled and puréed
    in a food processor
    or grated if you don't
    have a processor
6 cloves
2 cinnamon sticks
7 cloves garlic, crushed
    to a paste
6cm piece fresh ginger,
    peeled and grated
2 green chillies, split
    lengthways but still
    attached at the stalk
60g cashew nuts, toasted
    (optional)
250g baby leaf spinach
1 small bunch of coriander,
    chopped
salt and freshly ground
    black pepper

Place half the garam masala, chilli powder and turmeric in a large bowl along with a generous amount of salt and pepper. Add the lamb neck and mix so that the meat is well coated in the spices. Leave to one side.

Heat the oil in a large saucepan over a medium heat. When hot add the puréed onions and a pinch of salt. Fry the onions, stirring regularly for about 15 minutes by which time they should have coloured and become meltingly soft.

Add the cloves, cinnamon, garlic and ginger. Increase the heat a little, and fry, stirring regularly for a further 2–3 minutes, before adding the remainder of the ground spices and the green chillies. Fry for another minute. Increase the heat to maximum and tip in the marinated meat, scraping in any spices left in the dish. Fry for 2–3 minutes, stirring almost constantly. Pour in 500ml water, stirring as you add. Bring the liquid to the boil before reducing the heat and simmering the curry for about 1½ hours, adding a little water if it is looking dry.

Whilst the meat is cooking pour 100ml boiling water over the cashew nuts, if using, and leave for at least 10 minutes. Purée the nuts in the water using either a food processor or a pestle and mortar. Keep to one side.

After 1½ hours the meat should be tender, if not, continue to cook for a bit longer. Add the cashew purée and stir. Bring the curry back to the boil. Add the spinach and coriander. Your curry is ready as soon as the spinach has wilted.

TARKA DAL

SERVES 4

Lentils are the perfect vehicle for spice and deep flavours and as such offer a wonderful vegetarian alternative to the usual meat curry – not to mention the fact that they are kinder on your stomach. Think of this recipe as a base for experimentation; use the same cooking method and amounts but the spice combinations are only limited by your imagination.

**PREP TIME: 20 MINS,
PLUS SOAKING TIME
COOKING TIME: 1 HOUR**

250g yellow lentils
  (chana dal)
4 cloves garlic, finely diced
4cm piece fresh ginger,
  peeled and grated
1 tbsp ground turmeric
2 green chillies, split
  lengthways but still
  attached at the stalk
2 tomatoes, roughly chopped
2 tbsp vegetable or
  sunflower oil
1 red onion, finely diced
2 tsp black or yellow
  mustard seeds
about 24 curry leaves,
  or use 2 fresh bay leaves
  if unavailable
1 tbsp garam masala
juice of 1 lemon
1 small bunch of coriander,
  chopped
salt and freshly ground
  black pepper

Tip the lentils into a large bowl and cover with water. Soak in the water for 1 hour.

Strain the lentils through a sieve, washing them with fresh water. Place the lentils in a pan and cover with 1.5 litres of water. Bring to the boil over a high heat, skimming off any scum that rises to the top.

Add the garlic, ginger, turmeric, chillies and tomatoes. Simmer the lentils for about 50 minutes to 1 hour by which time they should be completely tender and falling apart. Stir the lentils vigorously with a wooden spoon to break them up, then set this mixture to one side.

Heat the oil in a frying pan over a medium-high heat. Add the onion and fry for 2 minutes before adding all of the remaining ingredients except the lemon juice and coriander. Fry, stirring almost constantly, for a further 3–4 minutes. Tip this mixture into the cooked lentils and stir through. Add a generous amount of salt and black pepper, then stir in the lemon juice and chopped coriander. Serve.

CHICKEN KORMA

SERVES 4-6

According to the British mindset, korma is the mildest type of curry. It's the one that people who don't like curry eat when they are forced into the local Indian restaurant by colleagues. I have taken what I consider to be the main flavourings of a korma; coconut, cardamom and almond; and have created a recipe complex enough for the curry lover but mild enough for the masses.

PREP TIME: 30 MINS
COOKING TIME: 30 MINS

2 large onions, roughly
    chopped into chunks
4 tbsp vegetable or
    sunflower oil
2 cinnamon sticks
6 green cardamom pods,
    lightly crushed with
    the side of a knife
1 long green chilli, split
    lengthways but still
    attached at the stalk
4cm piece fresh ginger,
    peeled and grated
5 cloves garlic, finely chopped
2 tbsp garam masala, plus
    a little extra for dusting
1 tbsp ground cumin
1 tbsp ground coriander
1 x 400ml tin coconut milk
4 large skinless chicken
    breasts, sliced in half
    widthways
60g raisins, soaked in warm
    water for 10 minutes,
    then drained
40g ground almonds
40g desiccated coconut
salt and freshly ground
    black pepper
Crispy Fried Shallots
    (see page 20), to serve
coriander leaves, to serve

Place the onions in a food processor along with a generous pinch of salt and blend until smooth. Warm the oil in a large, high-sided frying pan or saucepan over a medium-high heat. Add the puréed onion and fry, stirring regularly for about 15 minutes, until it is almost completely soft and lightly browned. It may be necessary to add a little more oil as you go.

Add the cinnamon, cardamom, green chilli, ginger and garlic and continue to stir and fry for 3 minutes. Spoon in the garam masala, cumin and coriander and continue to fry, stirring regularly for a further 2 minutes.

Pour in the coconut milk, bring to the boil, then reduce the heat and simmer for about 10 minutes, by which time the coconut milk should have reduced. Sprinkle your chicken pieces with a little garam masala as well as a generous grind of salt before dropping them into the simmering sauce. Bring the liquid back up to the boil, then simmer again and cook the chicken, stirring regularly for 5 minutes.

Sprinkle in the raisins, ground almonds and coconut and add 150ml water. Stir to combine. If at this point you feel the curry is a bit dry then keep on adding water until you are happy with the consistency.

Season the curry with salt and pepper and simmer for a further 5 minutes by which time the chicken should be fully cooked through. If unsure pick out the biggest piece of chicken and cut it open – it should be white all the way through. Serve with crispy fried shallots and coriander.

SLOW-COOKED LAMB BIRIYANI

SERVES 6

A classic biriyani is a multi-layered rice and meat dish. As delicious as it is, it is also laborious to make. Consider this as more of a single-storey, bungalow biriyani. The recipe may look complicated but once the lamb is in the oven it really is very easy and the resulting dish is resplendent in both taste and appearance – a worthy centrepiece to any table. Try this as an alternative to your Sunday lunch, served with Tomato and Tamarind Relish and naan bread and watch as children leave their toys and teenagers forget their phones for a brief, but delicious few moments.

PREP TIME: 30 MINS,
PLUS MARINATING TIME
COOKING TIME: ABOUT 4 HOURS

200g natural yoghurt
5cm piece fresh ginger,
    peeled and grated
8 cloves garlic, crushed
2 tbsp garam masala
1 tsp smoked paprika
2 tsp ground coriander
2 tsp ground turmeric
juice of 1 lemon
1 lamb shoulder, about 2kg
2 tbsp sunflower or vegetable oil
1 large onion, finely diced
8 cloves
6 green cardamom pods,
    lightly crushed with the
    side of a knife
2 bay leaves, fresh if possible
2 cinnamon sticks
400g basmati rice, rinsed
600ml chicken stock
3 large sprigs rosemary
salt and freshly ground
    black pepper
seeds of 1 pomegranate, to serve
1 small bunch of mint,
    leaves only, to serve
Tomato and Tamarind Relish
    (see page 15), to serve
naan bread, to serve

Place the yoghurt, ginger, garlic, ground spices and lemon juice in a bowl along with a generous amount of salt and pepper. Mix thoroughly with a spoon until you have a smooth marinade.

Take the lamb shoulder and using a small, sharp knife puncture the flesh in about 20 places. Smother the shoulder in the yoghurt marinade, ensuring you work it into the meat. Cover with cling film and leave to marinate in the fridge for a minimum of 6 hours or preferably overnight.

When ready to cook, remove the marinated meat from the fridge, uncover, and leave to warm a little whilst you wait for your oven to preheat to 230°C/220°C fan/ 450°F/gas mark 8.

Place the shoulder in a large roasting tin, then roast for 15 minutes, by which time the meat should have browned in a few places. Remove the lamb from the oven and pour 250ml boiling water into the base of the roasting tin. Reduce the oven temperature to 160°C/150°C fan/325°F/gas mark 3. Loosely cover the shoulder with some baking parchment, then cover the whole roasting tin with tin foil, and cook the lamb in the oven for 3½ hours.

CONTINUED OVERLEAF

When the lamb has about 20 minutes left of its cooking time, find a large, ovenproof dish that is big enough to fit the lamb in one piece (a deep roasting tray will do). Heat the oil in the ovenproof dish over a medium-high heat. Add the onion and fry, stirring regularly for 5 minutes or until the onion has softened and taken on a little colour. Add the cloves, cardamom, bay leaves and cinnamon. Continue frying and stirring for a further 3 minutes by which time your kitchen should be filled with heady and delicious aromas. Tip in the rice, and stir to coat in the oil and spices. Pour in the stock and bring to the boil. Add a generous sprinkle of salt to the pan, then place a piece of baking parchment over the rice.

The lamb should have had its requisite time by now, so remove from the oven and replace it with the rice. Cook the rice in the oven for 15 minutes before removing and discarding the parchment. Increase the oven temperature to 170°C/160°C fan/340°F/gas mark 3½.

Now to assemble: spoon a generous amount of the cooking juices from the bottom of the lamb roasting dish over the cooked rice, this will add colour and flavour. Next lay the rosemary sprigs randomly on top of the rice. Carefully pick up the lamb shoulder (a combination of tongs, a friend and a spatula works very well) and place on top of the rice. Place the lid on top of the dish and place back in the oven.

After 12 minutes remove the dish from the oven, and let it rest for 10 minutes. When ready to serve remove the lid and scatter over the pomegranate seeds and mint leaves for a final flourish. Serve with the chutney, naan bread and knowing pride. This is well worth the effort.

→ CHAPTER
TWO

CHINESE *

Chinese food is one of the world's favourite cuisines with takeaway restaurants a common sight almost everywhere. The fermented sauces such as soy, oyster and fish sauce hook people in with their almost addictive savoury taste. Mix in satisfying carbs like noodles and rice, toss them all together with onions and garlic in a scorching wok, and there is little wonder that Chinese fast food is so universally loved.

However, of all the cuisines Chinese is now probably the worst served by takeaways. Being one of the earliest foreign foods to be widely exported around the world it has had too much time to evolve and bow to the pressures of profit margin and laziness. Too many times I have eaten Chinese takeaway food that is just foil cartons filled with undercooked chunks of onions and indigestible peppers held together in a gloop of heavily flavoured sauce; the classic flavours of soy and garlic used to disguise rather than flavour.

I want you to cook the dishes in the following chapter just so you remember how good Chinese food really can be. At its best it is as fresh as any other country's offerings, the method of quickly stir-frying sealing in flavour whilst preserving the individual textures of ingredients. China is a vast land that offers such a huge variety of produce, techniques and flavours; my recipes only scratch the surface of one of the world's great cuisines. Use the following chapter as a springboard and catalyst to find out more.

SALT and PEPPER SQUID

SERVES 4

By the time the scooter driver arrives at your door, there is only the very slimmest chance that your squid will still be crispy. For as soon as fried squid is sealed in its takeaway container, humidity gets to work softening the batter. This makes salt and pepper squid a prime candidate to try at home, and believe me, once you have tried this recipe you will banish thoughts of ever ordering this dish from the takeaway again.

PREP TIME: 10 MINS
COOKING TIME: 5 MINS

- about 500ml of vegetable or sunflower oil, for shallow frying
- 6 large, fresh squid, cleaned and tentacles and body separated (ask your fishmonger to do this for you if you like)
- 100g cornflour
- 2 tsp salt
- 1tsp ground black pepper
- 2 tsp five spice powder
- 4 spring onions, trimmed and cut into 1cm slices
- 1 red chilli, roughly chopped (remove the seeds if you don't like the heat)
- 2 cloves garlic, finely chopped

Heat the oil to 180°C in a deep-sided frying pan or wok. If you don't have a thermometer then you can tell when the oil is at 180°C by dropping a cube of bread into it; the bread should turn golden brown in about 30 seconds.

Taking each squid body in turn slice the tube open and then slice the flesh into 2cm-thick pieces. If you have the stomach for it then slice the eyes away from the tentacles and add to your pile of prepared squid.

Tip the cornflour into a large bowl and add the salt, black pepper and five spice powder. Toss until well combined.

Tip the prepared squid into the bowl of seasoned cornflour and toss with your hands, ensuring the squid is evenly coated with the flour.

Carefully lower the squid pieces into the hot oil and fry for 2 minutes until lightly golden before removing with a slotted spoon on to a piece of kitchen paper. Don't overload your pan with squid, if need be cook the squid in batches.

When all of the squid is cooked, spoon a couple of tablespoons of the hot oil into a clean saucepan over a high heat. When hot add the spring onion, chilli and garlic. Fry, stirring almost constantly, for 2 minutes.

Toss the cooked squid in with the frying onion mix and toss to coat.

VEGETABLE SPRING ROLLS

MAKES 20 CANAPÉ-SIZED SPRING ROLLS

Even my gran knows what a spring roll is, that's how famous these crunchy cigars of joy are. They are also incredibly simple; so simple in fact that you can pretend to your children that helping you prepare enough for your dinner party is a fun way to spend the day. The rolls freeze very well once cooked, just ensure they cool completely before freezing on a tray lined with greaseproof paper. Serve hot or at room temperature with sweet chilli sauce.

PREP TIME: 20 MINS
COOKING TIME: 10 MINS

1 carrot, grated
5 spring onions, trimmed and finely sliced
4 cloves garlic, finely diced
1 red chilli, deseeded and finely sliced
¼ white cabbage, core removed and leaves very finely shredded
200g beansprouts
2 tbsp light soy sauce
5 spring roll wrappers (about 25 x 25cm)
about 1 litre sunflower or vegetable oil, for deep-frying
salt and freshly ground black pepper
sweet chilli sauce, to serve

Place the carrot, spring onions, garlic, chilli, white cabbage and beansprouts in a large bowl. Pour in the soy sauce along with a generous amount of salt and pepper. Give the ingredients a thorough mix with your hands.

To construct your spring rolls. Take one wrapper at a time and place on a chopping board. Use a sharp knife or scissors to cut the wrapper into 4 equal squares. Take one square, and place a heaped tablespoon of the mixture in a line across the middle of the square, leaving a 2cm border at each end of the filling. With a wet finger or a pastry brush generously moisten the edges.

Begin rolling your spring roll by bringing the two ends in over the filling. With fingers still holding the sides use your thumbs to pick up the edge closest to you, and fold over the filling. Tuck the edge under the pile of vegetables, and roll the pastry up into a fully enclosed cigar shape. Repeat the process with the remaining squares of pastry.

Heat the oil 180°C in a deep-sided saucepan or wok to. If you don't have a thermometer then you can tell when the oil is at 180°C by dropping a cube of bread into it; the bread should be golden brown in about 30 seconds.

Carefully lower a few spring rolls into the hot oil. Let them bubble away for about 4 minutes, by which time the wrapper will be perfectly cooked, crisp and golden. Drain the rolls on kitchen paper to remove excess oil. Repeat with remaining batches. Serve with sweet chilli sauce.

GRILLED SESAME PRAWN TOASTS

SERVES 2

This has to be one of the worst represented dishes on the Chinese takeaway menu. Too often you open your container to reveal greasy-spoon style fried bread, with a hint of prawn spread over the top, all topped with a concrete layer of sesame seeds. We seem to eat the toasts out of habit and a craving for that omni-flavoured oil that the toasts are fried (destroyed) in. Not only are these prawn toasts far healthier, they are so simple, yet so delicious you will find yourself wondering why you ever dialled the takeaway's number.

PREP TIME: 10 MINS
COOKING TIME: 6 MINS

**10 good-sized raw
   prawns, peeled**
**1 egg white, lightly whisked
   until just frothy**
1 tsp sesame oil
½ tbsp cornflour
1 tbsp light soy sauce
1 tbsp finely chopped chives
**1cm piece fresh ginger,
   peeled and grated**
1 clove garlic, finely diced
**2 thick slices of white
   bread, toasted**
about 2 tbsp sesame seeds
**Pickled Cucumbers
   (see page 44), to serve**

Place the prawns on your chopping board and using a sharp knife, mince them as finely as possible. This takes a bit of time, but is worth doing. You may be tempted to use a food processor, but I find doing it by hand results in a better texture. Place the minced prawns in a bowl along with the egg white, sesame oil, cornflour, soy sauce, chives, ginger and garlic. Mix all of the ingredients until they are thoroughly combined.

Preheat your grill to a medium-high heat.

Using a spoon or knife spread the prawn mixture on top of the toast, dividing it evenly. Spread right to the edges, and don't be afraid to spread it thickly. Sprinkle each piece with a generous amount of sesame seeds and place under the grill.

Grill the toasts for 5–6 minutes, by which time the sesame seeds should have turned a lovely golden colour and the prawn mixture should be cooked all the way through. If you are unsure if the prawn is cooked then cut a toast in the middle – the flesh should have turned a light shade of pink. Serve up your prawn toast with some pickled cucumbers.

PICKLED CUCUMBERS

SERVES 4 AS A SIDE DISH

This incredibly quick and easy side dish is the perfect foil to any plate of rich food. The subtle sweet and sour flavours punch well above their weight. These cucumbers will sit perfectly with many of the dishes from this chapter such as Grilled Sesame Prawn Toasts (see page 42), Pork and Aubergine Stew (see page 46) and Honey-roast Pork Belly (see page 64).

PREP TIME: 5 MINS
COOKING TIME: 0 MINS,
BUT AT LEAST 30 MINS'
PICKLING TIME

10 tbsp rice wine vinegar
2 tsp sugar
4 tsp salt
1 cucumber

Pour the rice wine vinegar into a bowl and add the sugar and salt. Mix the liquid vigorously until both the sugar and salt have completely dissolved into the liquid. Keep to one side.

Peel your cucumber. You don't have to be completely fastidious about this, a bit of skin is not a problem, and can add to the texture.

Slice the cucumber in half lengthways, then run a teaspoon down the core to remove the seeds. Chop the cucumber into batons about 5 x 1cm. Again, you don't have to be centimetre perfect.

Place the batons in a small bowl and pour over the vinegar mixture. Tumble the cucumbers about, so that they all pick up some of the seasoned vinegar. Leave the cucumbers to pickle for a minimum of 30 minutes, ensuring you mix them around every now and then.

The cucumbers can be left in their pickling liquid in the fridge for about 5 days. Just be aware that the longer they spend in the vinegar the more potent the flavour becomes, something I find delicious.

EGG-FRIED RICE

SERVES 4

This is very often the first item to be ordered at a Chinese restaurant and normally forms the base on to which you pile all the other dishes. It is best to use day-old rice for fried rice because it is drier. To ensure you don't poison anybody ensure you leave your freshly cooked rice to cool completely before covering and storing in the fridge until ready to use. The below recipe forms the foundation for you to add your own flavours, just remember that any raw ingredients go in before the rice and any cooked ones after the rice.

PREP TIME: 10 MINS
COOKING TIME: 10 MINS

3 eggs
3 tbsp light soy sauce
3 tsp sesame oil
3 tbsp sunflower or
    vegetable oil
1 onion, cut into 1cm dice
2 carrots, cut into 1cm dice
2 cloves garlic,
    finely chopped
150g frozen peas
275g plain rice, cooked
    according to the packet
    instructions then
    cooled completely
100ml Shaoxing rice wine
    or dry sherry
2 spring onions, finely sliced

Crack the eggs into a small bowl and add 1 tablespoon of the soy sauce along with 1 teaspoon of the sesame oil. Whisk the ingredients, ensuring they are well combined.

Heat 1 tablespoon of the oil in a large frying pan or wok over a high heat. When very hot pour in the seasoned egg mixture and allow to set and bubble up. If you're using a wok, then you may have to swill the egg around a bit. Let the egg fry for 1 minute before breaking it up with a wooden spoon, and continuing to fry for a further minute whilst continuing to break the egg into small, bite-sized pieces.

Tip the egg out on to a plate, wipe out your frying pan or wok and place back over the high heat. Pour in the remaining 2 tablespoons of oil and when hot add the onion and carrots and fry, stirring almost constantly, for 1 minute before adding the garlic. Continue to stir and fry for a further minute. Tumble in the frozen peas and leave to cook for 1 minute.

Pour in the rice and follow immediately with the Shaoxing wine. I like to use a combination of two wooden spoons to simultaneously break up the rice whilst stirring and mixing in with the already frying ingredients. Fry the ingredients for a further 2 minutes before returning the egg to the pan.

Pour in the remaining soy sauce and sesame oil and give the whole lot a couple more turns to ensure everything is well mixed and distributed. Serve up, topped with the spring onions, and watch your massive pile of fried rice disappear in less time than it took you to cook it.

PORK and AUBERGINE STEW

SERVES 4

This dish is one you may have passed over a thousand times when looking
at your local takeaway menu. It does not have the most alluring title, but it is
one of the greatest Chinese dishes ever made, and it is about time you tried
it. It is very easy to convert this stew to a vegetarian one. Simply remove
the pork, and increase the amount of tofu to about 300g.

PREP TIME: 10 MINS
COOKING TIME: 30 MINS

2 tbsp sunflower or
   vegetable oil
75g minced pork
6 spring onions, trimmed
   and finely sliced
4 cloves garlic, finely diced
2 large aubergines, stalk
   removed, chopped
   into 3cm chunks
5 tinned anchovies, drained
   and finely chopped
5 tbsp light soy sauce
250g firm tofu, chopped
   into 3cm chunks
2 tsp sesame oil
2 red chillies, deseeded and
   finely sliced, to garnish
1 tbsp sesame seeds,
   toasted, to garnish
Egg Fried Rice, to serve
   (see page 45)

Heat the oil in a large saucepan over a high heat. When
hot, add the pork and fry, stirring, for about 3 minutes,
by which time the meat should be nicely broken up.
At this point, if the meat has released a lot of fat it may
be necessary to drain most of it off.

Reduce the heat to medium-high and add the spring
onions and garlic. Fry for 1 minute before adding the
aubergines and continuing to fry, stirring regularly,
for a further 2 minutes.

Add the anchovies and 3 tablespoons of the soy sauce
along with 100ml of water. Bring the whole lot to the boil,
before reducing the heat to a simmer. Cover with a cocked
lid and cook for 20 minutes, by which time the aubergine
should be completely soft. Keep an eye on the amount
of liquid in the pan – it may be necessary to add a little
extra water every now and then.

Add the tofu chunks, replace the lid and continue to cook
for a further 5 minutes.

Pour in the remaining soy sauce and the sesame oil. Stir
to ensure all the ingredients are well combined.

Serve up your delicious aubergine dish garnished with
the chilli and sesame seeds, with egg fried rice on the side.

STIR-FRIED MUSHROOMS WITH PAK CHOI

SERVES 4

Chinese food is so badly represented by a great many takeaways you may never have really considered vegetables to be of much importance to Chinese cuisine. Often they seem to be no more than a colourful afterthought used to pad out gloopy sauces thin on meat. The opposite could not be more true, the Chinese are outstanding exponents of tasty veg. The method below could be used with almost all soft vegetables from courgettes to lettuce leaves.

PREP TIME: 10 MINS
COOKING TIME: 5 MINS

2 tbsp sunflower or vegetable oil
225g oyster mushrooms, torn into 2cm strips
1 large clove of garlic, peeled and finely diced
4 heads of pak choi, root removed, leaves separated
2 tbsp light soy sauce
2 tsp sesame oil

Pour the oil into a large frying pan or wok and heat until it is smoking hot. Add the mushrooms and fry for about 45 seconds by which time they will have browned lightly.

Add the garlic to the hot pan and continue to fry for a further 30 seconds, stirring. Drop in the pak choi and stir to mix it with the mushrooms. Pour in 3 tablespoons of water and continue to fry until the pak choi begins to wilt, this shouldn't take more than 1 minute. Remove the pan from the heat and pour in the soy sauce and sesame oil. Mix to ensure all the ingredients are evenly coated.

Serve up with a bowl of plain rice, or as an accompaniment to meat or fish.

CHICKEN and SWEETCORN SOUP

SERVES 2

I, like many others, have a bit of a love-hate relationship with this soup. I love it because it tastes great and is unlike any Western soup; but I also hate it, because I know that soup shouldn't resemble wallpaper paste like the takeaway version so often does! This recipe is brilliant for using up leftover roast chicken; you can pick the meat from the carcass, and then boil it up with a couple of peeled onions to make the requisite stock. If you do end up using shop-bought stock, try to buy the fresh stuff from the cooled section – it makes all the difference.

PREP TIME: 10 MINS
COOKING TIME: 8 MINS

1 tbsp sunflower
    or vegetable oil
1 clove garlic, finely chopped
2cm piece fresh ginger,
    peeled and grated
150g cooked chicken,
    shredded
200g tinned creamed
    sweetcorn
500ml chicken stock,
    ideally fresh
2 eggs
2 tbsp light soy sauce
1 tsp sesame oil
salt and freshly ground
    black pepper

Heat the oil in a medium saucepan over a medium heat. When hot, add the garlic and ginger. Fry for 1 minute, stirring regularly.

Add the chicken and continue to stir and fry for a further minute. Pour in the creamed sweetcorn and the stock, then bring the liquid to a boil, before reducing the heat and simmering for 5 minutes. Taste and season well with salt and pepper.

Crack the eggs into a bowl, pour in the soy sauce and whisk until they are well combined.

Use a large spoon to stir your still-simmering soup, and whilst continuing to stir, pour in the seasoned egg. Continue stirring the soup until it just comes back to the boil. At this point the egg will have separated into fine strings.

Stir in the sesame oil and give the soup one last taste, adding salt and pepper as necessary.

Serve up steaming bowls of your gorgeous, gloop-free soup.

PRAWN and BEANSPROUT FU YUNG

SERVES 1

Fu yung is essentially a soy-flavoured scrambled omelette to which you can add almost any leftovers that need using up. From cold meat to vegetables, the fried eggs and Chinese seasonings carry them all effortlessly. The most important thing to remember when cooking this dish is to brown the eggs. It is the combination of the seasoning and the light nutty flavour of browned eggs that is the key to a good fu yung.

PREP TIME: 5 MINS
COOKING TIME: 5 MINS

2 large eggs
1 tbsp soy sauce
2 tsp sesame oil
2 tbsp sunflower
   or vegetable oil
5 good-sized raw
   prawns, peeled
2 spring onions, trimmed –
   the white chopped into
   1cm pieces; the green
   finely sliced
50g beansprouts
a few sprigs of coriander
hot chilli sauce, to serve
   (optional)
freshly ground black pepper

Crack the eggs into a small bowl and pour in the soy sauce and sesame oil, along with a generous pinch of pepper. Keep the mixture to one side.

Heat 1 tablespoon of the oil in a small, non-stick frying pan over a medium-high heat. When hot drop in the prawns and fry, stirring occasionally for about 1 minute, until they just begin to brown. Add the whites of the spring onions and continue to fry for a further 30 seconds.

Pour in the remaining tablespoon of oil, and wait 10 seconds before pouring in the seasoned egg mixture. The egg should instantly bubble up around the edges. Leave the egg to fry like this for 30 seconds without stirring. Resist the urge to stir, even if you think the egg is burning! Begin to pull the edges of the egg into the middle, turning some of the egg as you go. You are aiming for large chunks of browned egg that are still a little soft in the middle – this should take about 2 minutes. It might take you a couple of attempts to perfect this, but the flavour is so good, you won't mind.

When you are happy with the eggs, add the beansprouts, and mix in quickly; you only want to warm the beansprouts through, no more.

Tip the cooked eggs on to a plate and dress with the coriander sprigs, green parts of the spring onions, and hot chilli sauce, if using.

GINGER STEAMED MONKFISH

SERVES 2

This recipe demonstrates the more subtle side of Chinese cooking. The flavours are bold, but well blended to accentuate, not mask the natural sweetness of the fish. Classically this recipe would be cooked in a steamer, but I have opted to wrap the ingredients in tin foil and cook in the oven to make it easier. Although I've chosen monkfish, almost any firm-fleshed fish, from salmon to pollock would work in the same way, just increase or decrease the cooking time depending on the thickness of the fish you use.

PREP TIME: 10 MINS
COOKING TIME: 10 MINS

2 tsp sunflower or
    vegetable oil
350g monkfish, trimmed and
    sliced into 2cm thick discs
3cm piece fresh ginger,
    peeled and sliced into
    matchsticks
4 spring onions, trimmed
    and finely sliced
2 tbsp soy sauce
2 tbsp Shaoxing rice wine
    or dry sherry
1 red chilli, deseeded and
    finely sliced
2 tsp sesame oil
½ tsp black sesame seeds
freshly cooked plain rice,
    to serve

Preheat your oven to 190°C/fan 180°C/375°F/gas mark 5.

Cut a sheet of tin foil roughly 40 x 20 cm. Cut a piece of baking parchment just a little smaller in size and lay on top of the foil.

Drizzle the oil into the middle of the baking parchment and spread a little using a small piece of parchment or your fingers. Arrange the discs of monkfish in a single layer in the middle of the parchment – overlapping a little is ok, stacking is not.

Scatter over half of the ginger and spring onions. Drizzle the soy sauce and Shaoxing wine over the ingredients. Draw the sides of the foil and parchment up over the raw ingredients and fold together all the way around the join to create a sealed parcel. Place your parcel on to a baking tray and slide into the oven. Bake for 10 minutes.

Remove the tray from the oven and let the parcel sit for 2 minutes. Carefully slice open the inflated package by cutting straight through the tin foil with a knife or scissors: pay close attention to the escaping steam as it could scald you. Pull back the sides of your package and scatter the remaining ginger, spring onions and the chilli over the top of the cooked fish. Finish with a scattering of black sesame seeds and a drizzle of sesame oil. Serve with rice.

CHICKEN CHOW MEIN

SERVES 4

There was a time when fresh egg noodles were the provenance of specialist stores, however you can now find them in the fridge compartment of most supermarkets. If your supermarket hasn't quite caught up then use the dried version, following the package instructions for rehydrating. Use this recipe as a template; it works just as well with pork or prawns as it does with chicken. Also feel free to add other vegetables such as peppers, green beans or pak choi.

PREP TIME: 10 MINS
COOKING TIME: 8 MINS

2 large chicken breasts,
    cut into 1cm strips
4 tbsp light soy sauce
2 tbsp sunflower or
    vegetable oil
3 cloves garlic, finely sliced
2cm piece fresh ginger,
    peeled and finely chopped
1 large red onion, cut into
    about 8 thin wedges
100g mangetout, cut
    in half widthways
400g fresh egg noodles
3 tbsp Shaoxing rice wine
    or dry sherry
2 tsp sesame oil
4 spring onions, trimmed
    and finely sliced

Place the chicken breasts in a small bowl and pour in 2 tablespoons of the soy sauce, mix and leave to sit for 5 minutes.

When ready to cook heat the oil in a large frying pan or wok over a high heat. When hot add the garlic, ginger and red onion. Fry the vegetables for 2 minutes, stirring almost constantly.

Add the chicken slices, pouring in any of the soy sauce that is in the bowl too. Continue to fry, stirring regularly for 3–4 minutes. Tip in the mangetout, and stir-fry for a further minute before adding the egg noodles. Mix everything together – it may be useful to use a combination of two wooden spoons for this. Pour in the rice wine and let it bubble up and steam, you want it to almost completely evaporate. Mix again using your two wooden spoons, then remove the pan from the heat and stir in the remaining soy sauce and the sesame oil.

Scatter the noodles with the spring onions before serving.

SWEET *and* SOUR PORK BALLS

SERVES 4

Meltingly soft and tasty pork shoulder encased in a crisp batter, perched on a punchy sauce of sweet and sour flavours – it is not surprising that this is one of the Chinese takeaways' most ordered dishes. This recipe calls for fresh pineapple, however sometimes pineapples can be quite unripe, in which case it is best just to plump for the tinned version. Also if you don't want to use lager for your batter, then it is easily substituted with sparkling water, and if you don't have any of that to hand, then you can just about get by with tap water.

PREP TIME: 30 MINS
COOKING TIME: 25 MINS

2 tbsp sunflower or vegetable
   oil, plus about 1 litre
   for deep-frying
2 red onions, each chopped
   into 8 wedges
2 red peppers, deseeded and
   chopped into 2cm chunks
3 cloves garlic, finely sliced
4cm piece fresh ginger,
   peeled and grated
3 tbsp caster sugar
6 tbsp red wine vinegar
3 tomatoes, stem removed,
   each roughly chopped into 8
½ pineapple (about 200g),
   peeled and chopped into
   2cm chunks, or 200g tinned
   pineapple chunks, drained
2 tbsp light soy sauce
1 tbsp sesame oil
150g self-raising flour
75g cornflour, plus a little
   extra for dusting
orion salt
300ml lager
500g pork shoulder, chunks
   of fat removed, roughly
   chopped into 2cm chunks
salt and freshly ground
   black pepper
small bunch of coriander
   sprigs, to serve

Heat the 2 tablespoons of oil in a large frying pan over a medium-high heat. When hot add the red onions and peppers. Fry, stirring regularly, for 2 minutes, by which time the onion should be beginning to wilt. Add the garlic and ginger and continue to fry for a further minute.

Add the sugar, and continue to fry, stirring almost continuously, for about 30 seconds, by which time the sugar should have melted and started to caramelise. Pour in the vinegar and mix to combine with the rest of the ingredients. Add about 3 tablespoons of water to the pan at this point to create the start of a sauce.

Reduce the heat to medium and add the tomatoes. Cook for a minute before adding the pineapple. Continue to cook the ingredients for another 2 minutes before turning off and stirring through the soy sauce and sesame oil. Keep the sauce to one side.

Preheat the litre of oil in a deep-sided saucepan or wok to 180°C. If you don't have a thermometer then you can tell when the oil is at 180°C by dropping a cube of bread into it; the bread should be golden brown in about 30 seconds.

Tip the self-raising flour and cornflour into a bowl. Pour in the lager, whisking continuously, until it is fully incorporated and you have a batter that is the consistency of double cream.

Season the pork chunks with salt and pepper. Dust with a light coating of cornflour, before dunking them into the batter. Carefully lower a few pieces of coated meat into the hot oil. It is important not to overcrowd your oil with frying meat – if you do it will reduce the temperature of the oil, which will prevent the batter crisping and will result in soggy specimens. Cook in batches, keeping the fried meat warm in a low oven or grill.

Fry the pork for about 4 minutes, by which time the batter should have turned golden and the meat be fully cooked through. Drain on kitchen paper.

When ready to serve, heat the sauce, spoon on to a serving plate and top with the fried pork. Garnish with coriander sprigs and serve.

EASY CRISPY DUCK

This is a cheat's version of a dish that is incredibly quick and easy to make. The most important part of this recipe is cooking the duck breast from cold, which helps render the fat (melt and release it from the breast), creating a lovely crisp skin.

PREP TIME: 10 MINS
COOKING TIME: 16 MINS

2 duck breasts, patted dry
1 tsp five spice powder
2 tsp fine salt
1 tbsp sunflower or
**   vegetable oil**
½ cucumber, deseeded
**   and chopped into batons**
5 spring onions, trimmed
**   and finely sliced**
hoisin sauce, to serve
Chinese pancakes, to serve

Put the duck breasts skin-side down into a dry frying pan over a medium-high heat. As the pan heats, the fat will begin to melt and collect in the pan – tip out the excess fat as it forms.

Leave the breasts to cook for 8–10 minutes, by which time they should be deeply golden and crisp, so flip them over. If the skin is not crisp, continue cooking until it is. When you are happy with the duck breasts, remove them from the pan and carefully wipe the pan clean with some kitchen paper.

Mix the five spice powder and salt and use to season the duck breasts all over. Heat the oil in the frying pan over a medium-high heat, then return the duck to the pan, flesh-side down. Fry the breasts for a further 4 minutes, before flipping them on to the skin side again and cooking for another 2 minutes. Remove the breasts from the pan, and leave to rest for at least 4 minutes.

Whilst the duck is resting, set out all the garnishes – cucumber, spring onion and hoisin sauce – and warm your pancakes. I find the best way to do this is in the microwave but if you don't have one you can gently steam them wrapped in baking parchment and then in tin foil. When ready to serve, cut the duck breasts into thin slices, and serve to your nearest and dearest.

HONEY-ROAST PORK BELLY

SERVES 4

This recipe cooks the belly twice, once to imbue it with flavour and again to lacquer the meat in a glorious, caramelised coating of honey. Go forth and enjoy. This recipe works equally well for ribs, just cut down the cooking times by about half.

PREP TIME: 14 MINS
COOKING TIME: 2 HOURS 30 MINS

2kg pork belly, in one piece
   if possible, rind on
4 rashers of smoked streaky
   bacon, roughly chopped
2 onions, roughly chopped
3 star anise
10cm piece fresh ginger,
   peeled and grated
10 cloves garlic, peeled
   and bashed with the
   palm of your hand
250ml Shaoxing rice wine
   or dry sherry
250ml light soy sauce
100g clear honey
5 spring onions, trimmed
   and finely sliced
freshly cooked rice,
   preferably jasmine,
   to serve

Place the pork belly in a large saucepan. Add the bacon, onions, star anise, ginger, garlic, Shaoxing wine and soy sauce. Pour enough water into the pan to cover the pork belly by at least 10cm.

Place the pan over a high heat and bring the liquid to the boil, skimming off any scum that rises to the surface. Reduce the heat so that the liquid is just simmering – this means a few 'burping' bubbles every now and then, not rolling bubbles. Cook the pork like this for 2 hours.

The pork should now be meltingly soft. Remove from the heat and allow the meat to cool to room temperature in the liquid.

Preheat your oven to 200°C/190°C fan/400°F/gas mark 6. Line a roasting tray with tin foil (this is to save your pan – you will thank me later).

Carefully remove the pork from the cooking liquor. Use a sharp knife to remove the soft rind, which can be discarded.

Place the joint of meat on to the lined tray and pour over the honey. Roast in the oven for 15 minutes, then remove and flip the meat over, spooning over the bubbling honey as you do so. Roast for a further 10 minutes, before removing to baste again. Flip the joint again and roast for a final 10 minutes. You should now be looking at a gloriously glossy, perfectly cooked piece of meat. Chop the meat into large chunks, scatter with the spring onions and serve with rice.

CHAPTER THREE

* **THAI** →

Thai cuisine is packed to the gunnels with flavour. In their culinary repertoire the Thais have some of the most pungent dishes created from perfectly balanced combinations of sweet, savoury, spicy and sour ingredients. Eating a Thai meal invigorates the mouth and gets the blood pumping; the flavours are so bold and lively they virtually hop, skip and jump all around the head, leaving you buzzing.

Careful flavouring is key when cooking Thai food because ingredients such as bird's-eye chillies are very potent. Make sure to taste your meals constantly as you prepare them, especially just before serving; Thai food is very forgiving and it is almost never too late to add a dash of sour lime juice or savoury fish sauce to bolster the flavour in a particular direction.

Although it is now very easy to find most Thai ingredients in mainstream supermarkets, you might find it more of a challenge to source some of the fresher, or more specialist ingredients. Do not worry as they can be replicated using other ingredients and a little creative thinking; I've given suggestions for suitable substitutions throughout the chapter.

SPICY BEEF SALAD

SERVES 2

Thailand offers an abundance of salads that feel both light and filling
at the same time. Maybe this is down to the robustness of the seasonings,
which do such a great job of satisfying the taste buds. This salad is the perfect
example; it uses a very small amount of meat, which, when dressed with
a heady mix of fish sauce, vinegar, shallots and chilli becomes very much
more than just a salad – it is pure gastronomic synergy. For this dish
you can use any steak but I prefer sirloin for flavour and texture.

PREP TIME: 15 MINS
COOKING TIME: 6 MINS,
PLUS RESTING TIME

1 tbsp vegetable oil
1 x 250g sirloin steak
2 tbsp red wine vinegar
1 tbsp fish sauce
2 tsp toasted sesame oil
1 large shallot, sliced
   into thin rings
1 bird's-eye chilli, finely
   chopped (remove
   the seeds if you don't
   like heat)
½ cucumber, halved
   lengthways, deseeded
   and chopped into
   5mm slices
2 heads little gem lettuce,
   leaves separated
½ small bunch of mint,
   leaves only
½ small bunch of coriander,
   leaves only
50g cashew nuts, toasted
salt and freshly ground
   black pepper
prawn crackers, to serve

Heat the oil in a frying pan over a high heat. Season the
steak with salt and pepper. When the oil is hot, carefully
lay the steak in the pan. Fry for about 4 minutes on each
side before removing it to a plate and leaving it to rest
for a minimum of 10 minutes for a medium-rare steak.

Mix the vinegar, fish sauce, sesame oil, shallot and red
chilli. Pour the dressing over the prepared cucumber
pieces and leave to macerate for 5 minutes.

When you are ready to serve your salad, drop the lettuce
leaves into a large bowl and tip in the macerated cucumber
pieces. Toss the ingredients together so that the leaves are
lightly coated in the dressing. Divide the dressed salad
between two plates.

Slice the steak into thin strips and place on top of the
salad. Finish by scattering over the herbs and nuts, then
crumbling over a few prawn crackers.

PAD THAI

SERVES 2

Satisfying rice stick noodles coated in a harmonious combination of sweet, salty and hot sauce and topped off with crunchy peanuts and beansprouts. But cliché or not, this dish stands the test of time because it so deliciously satisfying.

PREP TIME: 15 MINS
COOKING TIME: 10 MINS

**6 nests of dried rice
    noodles (90g)**
3 tbsp vegetable oil
**2 tbsp tamarind sauce
    or lime juice**
**1 tbsp grated palm sugar
    or agave syrup**
1 tbsp fish sauce
2 eggs
**3 tinned anchovies,
    finely chopped**
**10 raw king prawns, peeled
    apart from the very tip
    of the tail**
**3 spring onions,
    trimmed and sliced
    into 1cm pieces**
**1 red chilli, finely chopped
    (remove the seeds if you
    don't like too much heat)**
100g beansprouts
**3 tbsp salted peanuts,
    roughly chopped**
3–4 sprigs of coriander
**salt and freshly ground
    black pepper**
lime wedges, to serve

Rehydrate your noodles according to the packet instructions and drain through a fine sieve. Tip the noodles into a bowl, pour over 1 tablespoon of the vegetable oil and mix thoroughly with your hands to help stop clumping.

Put the tamarind sauce, sugar and fish sauce into a bowl and mix well until combined.

Crack the eggs into a small bowl, season with a little salt and pepper and whisk together.

Heat 1 tablespoon of the oil in a large frying pan over a high heat. When the oil is hot tip in the beaten eggs and fry, stirring regularly for about 2 minutes, by which time all of the egg should be fully cooked through. Tip the cooked egg on to a plate, and place the frying pan back over a high heat.

Pour in the final tablespoon of oil into the pan. When hot add the anchovy and stir-fry for 10 seconds before adding the prawns. Fry the prawns, turning occasionally for 1 minute. Add half the spring onions, along with the chilli, and continue to stir and fry for 1 minute before tipping in the noodles.

Toss the noodles in the pan to mix with the cooking ingredients. If you find the noodles are sticking together then add a drop of water. Continue to fry and toss until you are happy that the prawns are cooked through and the noodles warm.

Pour in the tamarind mixture and stir through the noodles until the sauce is evenly distributed. Add the beansprouts and give everything one final toss. Divide the noodles between two bowls and top with the peanuts and coriander, with lime wedges on the side.

PRAWN and TOASTED RICE SALAD

SERVES 2

This salad will set your mouth alight with delicious chilli and ginger, but then, in an instant, cool you back down with mellow cucumber and sweet mango. Add juicy prawns and crunchy toasted rice and you have a dish that will more than satisfy every taste receptor you have in your mouth.

PREP TIME: 20 MINS
COOKING TIME: 3 MINS

30g long-grain rice
juice of 3 limes
1 tbsp fish sauce
1 tsp toasted sesame oil
2 tsp palm sugar, grated,
    or agave syrup
1 stalk lemongrass, trimmed
    and finely chopped
2cm piece fresh ginger,
    peeled and minced
1 red chilli, finely diced
    (remove the seeds if you
    don't like too much heat)
2 spring onions, trimmed
    and finely sliced
220g cooked, peeled
    king prawns
1 mango, peeled and chopped
    into chunks (even unripe
    mango works here)
2 heads little gem lettuce,
    leaves separated
¼ cucumber, halved
    lengthways, deseeded and
    chopped into 5mm slices
½ small bunch of mint,
    leaves only

Tip the rice into a dry frying pan and place over a high heat. Cook, stirring regularly, for about 3 minutes. The rice is ready when it has turned a dark golden colour all over. Keep an eye on it as when it starts to colour it changes quickly. When evenly browned, scrape the rice on to a plate and leave to cool.

Place the lime juice in a bowl and add the fish sauce, sesame oil, sugar, lemongrass, ginger, red chilli and spring onions. Stir until the palm sugar dissolves into the liquid.

Tip the cooked prawns into a bowl and add the mango, lettuce leaves and cucumber. Add about three-quarters of the lime juice dressing and mix to coat the salad.

Use a pestle and mortar to lightly crush your toasted rice. If you don't have a pestle and mortar you can use a combination of a mug and a rolling pin.

Divide your dressed salad between two plates, and top with mint leaves and the crushed toasted rice. Sit back and enjoy the explosion of flavours.

FRAGRANT NOODLE *and* VEGETABLE SOUP

❋

SERVES 4

This soup is a great example of bold Thai flavours acting as an invigorator and balm. It is packed with fiery, yet clean flavours that when combined with crunchy vegetables and soft noodles break through the drudgery of any day and enliven mind, body and soul.

PREP TIME: 10 MINS
COOKING TIME: 8 MINS

1 litre vegetable stock
4cm piece fresh ginger, peeled and roughly chopped
2 stalks lemongrass, trimmed and very finely sliced
1 bird's-eye chilli, finely chopped, seeds removed if you don't like the heat
4 nests of dried egg noodles, cooked according to the packet instructions and cooled
2 tsp sesame oil
1 large carrot, chopped into matchsticks
80g beansprouts, rinsed
75g green beans, trimmed
2 tbsp light soy sauce
juice of lime, plus extra wedges to serve
3 tbsp salted peanuts, roughly chopped
½ small bunch of coriander, roughly chopped

Pour the vegetable stock into a large saucepan and add the ginger, lemongrass and chilli. Bring the liquid to the boil, then reduce the heat and simmer for about 5 minutes.

In the meantime divide the cooked egg noodles between two bowls. Drizzle a teaspoon of sesame oil over the stacked noodles. Divide the carrot, beansprouts and green beans between the two bowls – I like to stack all the ingredients on top of each other.

Remove the flavoured stock from the heat and stir in the soy sauce along with the lime juice. Pour the stock over the noodles and vegetables.

Top the dish with peanuts and coriander and serve with lime wedges for an additional sour kick.

SALMON TOM YUM

SERVES 2

This recipe is based on the classic Thai soup, tom yum. It is a steaming bowl of broth filled with everything that is good and proper about Thai food; robust sweet and savoury flavours amplified by hot chillies riding on the back of mild chicken stock. Cook up this recipe when you are a little under the weather, sit back and wait for the fiery flavours to blast away almost any common malady.

PREP TIME: 15 MINS
COOKING TIME: 30 MINS

1 litre chicken stock
1 stalk lemongrass, trimmed and roughly chopped
½ small bunch of coriander, stalks separated
2 fresh kaffir lime leaves
4 tomatoes, core removed and the flesh roughly chopped
2 bird's-eye chillies, split lengthways (remove the seeds if you don't like heat)
6cm piece fresh ginger, peeled and thinly sliced
juice of 1 lime
2 tbsp fish sauce
2 spring onions, trimmed and finely sliced
4 chestnut mushrooms, finely sliced
150g tenderstem broccoli, blanched for 30 seconds
200g skinless salmon fillet, sliced into 1cm pieces

Pour the stock into a saucepan and add the lemongrass, coriander stalks, lime leaves, tomatoes, chillies and ginger. Bring the ingredients to the boil before reducing the heat to a simmer.

After 20 minutes, strain the liquid through a fine sieve into a clean saucepan. Discard the ingredients in the sieve.

Bring the strained liquid back to the boil and add the lime juice and fish sauce.

Divide the spring onions, mushrooms, broccoli and salmon pieces between two bowls. Pour the boiling stock over the ingredients, and allow the soup to sit for 1 minute before serving.

STEAMED MUSSELS in COCONUT MILK

SERVES 2

The sweet plump flesh of cooked mussels has a wonderful way of absorbing the strong tastes of Thai ingredients, but it is the way the cooking liquor released from the steaming shellfish blends with the creamy broth that elevates this dish to a heavenly place.

PREP TIME: 15 MINS
COOKING TIME: 10 MINS

1kg fresh mussels
2 tbsp vegetable oil
2 shallots, finely diced
2 cloves garlic,
    finely chopped
1 small stalk lemongrass,
    trimmed and
    finely chopped
3cm piece fresh ginger,
    peeled and minced
1 red chilli, deseeded
    and finely sliced
1 kaffir lime leaf,
    finely shredded
250ml coconut milk
1 tbsp fish sauce
juice of 2 limes
½ small bunch of coriander,
    roughly chopped
freshly cooked rice,
    to serve

Clean the mussels. Place them in a bowl of cold water and scrub them well to remove any sand and grit. Pull off any beards (the stringy part) and give any open mussels a sharp tap, discarding any that don't close.

Heat the oil in a large saucepan over a medium-high heat. When hot add the shallots, garlic, lemongrass, ginger, chilli and lime leaf. Cook the ingredients, stirring regularly for 2 minutes.

Increase the heat to high and add the coconut milk. Bring the mixture to a boil and let it boil vigorously for 2–3 minutes by which time the liquid will have reduced by about a quarter. Add half of the fish sauce.

Drop the prepared mussels into the boiling liquid and immediately clamp the lid on top of the pan. Leave the mussels to cook for 3 minutes before removing the lid and having a look. If almost all of the mussels have opened then the dish is ready. If there are quite a few that are still shut, replace the lid and continue to cook for another minute.

When the mussels are cooked remove them from the heat, discard any that haven't opened, and pour in the remaining fish sauce, then the lime juice. Give the mussels one final stir before topping with the coriander and serving with rice.

CHICKEN and CASHEW NUTS

SERVES 4

Whether Chinese, Thai or Vietnamese, chicken and cashew is very often the go-to dish if you don't recognise anything else on the menu. The combination of chicken and cashew nuts is so perfect and so comforting. This is an extremely quick and easy dish to make – you may even find that it becomes a weekly staple.

PREP TIME: 10 MINS
COOKING TIME: 10 MINS

2 tbsp dark soy sauce
1 tbsp agave syrup
1 tbsp fish sauce
80g cashew nuts
2 tbsp vegetable oil
1 star anise
1 dried chipotle chilli or
   1 tsp dried chilli flakes
1 onion, roughly chopped
   into chunks
800g chicken breasts
   (about 4), chopped
   into 3cm chunks
2 green peppers, deseeded
   and chopped into
   2cm chunks
3 cloves garlic, finely
   chopped
2 spring onions, trimmed
   and finely sliced, to serve
1 small bunch of coriander,
   to serve
freshly cooked rice, to serve

Pour the soy sauce, agave syrup and fish sauce into a small bowl and mix well to combine.

Heat a large frying pan over a medium-high heat. When hot add the cashew nuts and dry-fry them, turning a couple of times for about 1 minute or until they are lightly browned. Tip the nuts out of the pan and leave to one side.

Pour the oil into the same frying pan over a high heat. When hot, add the star anise, chipotle chilli and onion and stir-fry the ingredients for 1 minute. Add the chicken and fry with the onion and star anise, stirring regularly for 2 minutes.

Add the peppers and garlic, and fry all the ingredients together, stirring regularly for 2 minutes. Pour in the soy mixture and let the ingredients come to the boil. Finally stir in the toasted cashew nuts.

Serve up your chicken and cashew nuts topped with the spring onions and coriander alongside freshly cooked rice.

MASSAMAN BEEF CURRY

❀

This deeply spiced curry is a delicious departure from the citrus-flavoured heat you would usually associate with Thai food. The inclusion of ground spices means that Massaman curry has much in common with the curries of the Indian subcontinent, where many believe it originates. Add to these spices the fresh flavours of lemongrass, lime and coconut and this truly is a curry to savour. This recipe uses beef, but lamb or pork work just as well; just make sure you choose a cut such as shoulder or leg to stand up to the long cooking time and ensure meltingly tender chunks of meat.

PREP TIME: 20 MINS
COOKING TIME: 1 HOUR 30 MINS

1 large onion, roughly diced
2 red chillies, deseeded
  and roughly chopped
4 cloves garlic,
  roughly chopped
2 stalks lemongrass,
  trimmed and
  roughly chopped
4cm piece fresh ginger,
  peeled and roughly
  chopped
juice of 2 limes
1 x 400ml tin coconut milk
2 tsp turmeric
2 tbsp mild curry powder
3 tbsp vegetable oil
1 cinnamon stick
2 star anise
1kg beef shin, chopped
  into 3cm cubes
300ml beef or chicken stock
2 potatoes, peeled and
  chopped into 3cm chunks
80g desiccated coconut
salt and freshly ground
  black pepper
coriander, to serve
  (optional)
freshly cooked rice,
  to serve

Place the onion, chillies, garlic, lemongrass, ginger, lime juice, half the coconut milk, the turmeric and curry powder into a food processor along with a generous amount of salt and pepper. Blitz the mixture until smooth.

Heat the oil in a large saucepan over a medium-high heat. When hot add the cinnamon stick and star anise and fry, stirring constantly, for 10 seconds. Pour in the blitzed curry mixture and fry the ingredients, stirring regularly for 5 minutes. The liquid will reduce.

Stir in the beef and continue to stir and fry for 30 seconds. Pour in the remaining coconut milk along with the stock. Bring the liquid to the boil before reducing to a simmer and cooking for 1 hour 20 minutes. Add the potatoes and continue to cook for about 10 minutes by which time the potatoes and meat should both be very tender. You are aiming to reduce the liquid in the curry to almost nothing by the end of the cooking process, but depending on how quickly you boil the curry it may be necessary to intermittently add a little water to avoid cooking the curry 'dry'.

When both the meat and potatoes are tender stir in the desiccated coconut. The coconut will absorb a lot of the liquid and turn the curry quite dry – this is perfect.

Serve up your curry with a scattering of coriander, if liked, and a steaming bowl of rice. Relax into what is one of the world's most comforting dishes.

THAI FRIED RICE

SERVES 4

Fried rice is one of the best methods of using up leftovers. When you have a fridge filled with limp vegetables and pieces of cooked meat, fry some rice with a chopped onion and throw the whole lot in. The classic Thai flavourings of lime and fish sauce make it markedly different from the Chinese version. Rice cooked the day before works best because it is drier; just be sure to allow your rice to cool completely before storing in the fridge.

PREP TIME: 15 MINS
COOKING TIME: 10 MINS

3 eggs
2 tbsp light soy sauce
2 tsp sesame oil
3 tbsp vegetable oil
1 large onion, finely diced
1 carrot, peeled finely diced
3 cloves garlic, finely sliced
100g frozen peas
400g cooked and cooled rice
220g cooked, peeled
  king prawns
1 tbsp ketjap manis
1 tbsp fish sauce
juice of 2 limes
salt and freshly ground
  black pepper
50g salted peanuts, roughly
  chopped, to garnish
1 small bunch of coriander,
  roughly chopped,
  to garnish

Crack the eggs into a bowl. Add 1 tablespoon of the soy sauce, and 1 teaspoon of the sesame seed oil along with a pinch of salt and pepper. Whisk the ingredients together.

Heat 1 tablespoon of the vegetable oil in a small non-stick frying pan over a high heat. When the oil is very hot pour in the whisked egg. Cook the egg for 1 minute on each side, by which time it should be completely cooked and browned in patches. Slide the egg from the pan on to a chopping board and dab lightly with kitchen paper to remove excess oil. Roll the omelette up like a cigar, then slice into 1cm-thick strips. Leave to one side.

Heat the remaining 2 tablespoons of oil in a large frying pan over a medium-high heat. When hot add the onion and carrot. Fry the vegetables, stirring regularly for 2 minutes before adding the garlic and continuing to stir and fry for 1 minute more.

Increase the heat to high and add the frozen peas. Fry the peas for 30 seconds before adding the rice. I like to use a combination of two wooden spoons to turn the rice in the hot oil and vegetables until all the ingredients are well mixed. Fry the rice for 1 minute. Tumble in the cooked prawns and sliced omelette and stir.

Pour in the remaining soy sauce and sesame oil and add the ketjap manis and fish sauce. Stir so that all the ingredients are seasoned evenly. Remove the pan from the heat and add the lime juice. Garnish the dish with the peanuts and coriander to serve.

GREEN CHICKEN CURRY

This is the best known of all Thai dishes. I am guessing it is so ubiquitously popular because each satisfying mouthful leads you greedily into the next one. Every bite and every slurp feels like a new flavour discovery, be it lime and lemongrass tap dancing on the tongue or fiery ginger and chillies catching you at the back of the palate. Thai green curry is about as exciting and enlivening a meal as there is anywhere in the world. To adjust a famous saying, if you are bored of Thai green curry then you are bored of life.

PREP TIME: 20 MINS
COOKING TIME: 25 MINS

2 stalks lemongrass,
    trimmed and finely sliced
4 large shallots,
    roughly chopped
5 cloves garlic,
    roughly chopped
5cm piece fresh ginger,
    peeled and roughly
    chopped
1–2 bird's-eye chillies
    (depending on how hot
    you like your curry),
    roughly chopped
1 bunch of coriander, leaves
    and stalks separated
2 tsp ground cumin
3 limes
2 tbsp vegetable oil
2 star anise
1 x 400ml tin coconut milk
400ml chicken stock
1 aubergine, trimmed and
    chopped into 2cm cubes
800g chicken breasts
    (about 4), chopped
    into 3cm chunks
2 tbsp fish sauce
1 small bunch of basil, leaves
    only, roughly chopped
salt and freshly ground
    black pepper
freshly cooked rice, to serve

Place the lemongrass, shallots, garlic, ginger, chillies, coriander stalks, ground cumin, the juice and grated zest of 1 of the limes in a small food processor along with a generous amount of salt and pepper and blitz until as smooth as possible. If you don't have a food processor you can use a pestle and mortar.

Heat the vegetable oil in a large saucepan over a medium heat. When hot add the star anise, and cook for 30 seconds before spooning in the blitzed ingredients. Fry the ingredients, stirring regularly for 5 minutes. Pour in the coconut milk and bring to a boil, then reduce the heat and simmer for 10 minutes, stirring regularly – the coconut milk will reduce by about half.

Pour in the stock and bring the liquid back to the boil. Add the aubergine and chicken and simmer gently for 10 minutes until you are happy that the chicken is fully cooked through. If you are not sure if the chicken is cooked or not simply remove one of the larger pieces and chop in half – the chicken should be white all the way through.

Stir in the fish sauce and the juice from the two remaining limes. Roughly chop the coriander leaves and add to the curry along with the basil. Serve up ladlefuls of steaming curry accompanied by rice and wait for the party to kick off in your mouth.

RED BEEF CURRY

SERVES 4

The difference between Thai green and red curry is the colour and amount of chillies used to make the curry paste. Where green is made with the slightly milder green chilli, the red curry tends to be the hotter brother, packed with spicy red bird's-eye chillies. As much as I respect tradition, I also respect the longevity of your taste buds, so for this reason I have foregone the bushel of chillies and have coloured and sweetened the flavour of the curry with roasted red peppers. This is not stictly authentic but it is definitely delicious.

PREP TIME: 20 MINS
COOKING TIME: 2 HOURS

2 stalks lemongrass,
    trimmed and finely sliced
4 cloves garlic, roughly chopped
2 roasted red peppers from a jar,
    deseeded and roughly chopped
4 large shallots,
    roughly chopped
4cm piece fresh ginger,
    roughly chopped
1 bunch of coriander, leaves
    and stalks separated
2 red bird's-eye chillies
    (depending on how hot
    you like your curry),
    roughly chopped
2 limes
2 tbsp vegetable oil
1.25kg beef shin or stewing beef,
    chopped into 3cm chunks
1 star anise
1 x 400ml tin of coconut milk
750ml beef stock
2 tbsp fish sauce
1 small bunch of basil,
    roughly chopped
salt and freshly ground
    black pepper
freshly cooked rice, to serve
tomato and lettuce salad,
    to serve

Place the lemongrass, garlic, peppers, shallots, ginger, coriander stalks, chillies and the grated zest and juice of 1 of the limes into a small food processor along with a generous amount of salt and pepper. Blitz the ingredients until they become a paste. If you don't own a food processor then use a pestle and mortar to grind the ingredients to a chunky paste.

Heat the oil in a large saucepan over a high heat. Season the pieces of beef, and add them to the hot oil. Fry for 2 minutes, stirring very occasionally – it is not imperative to brown all the pieces of meat for this recipe so don't worry about overloading the pan.

Reduce the heat to medium-high and add the blitzed ingredients and star anise to the pan. Continue to fry, stirring regularly, for 5 minutes. Pour in the coconut milk and bring to the boil. Reduce the heat to a simmer and let the liquid bubble away for about 5 minutes by which time much of the milk will have been absorbed or evaporated.

Pour in the stock and bring the liquid back to the boil, then reduce to a simmer. Cook the curry for about 1½ hours, by which time the beef should be meltingly tender. If it isn't just leave it to simmer until you're happy with it.

Stir in the fish sauce, basil and the juice of the remaining lime, then serve with the rice and a small tomato and lettuce salad.

★ CHAPTER
FOUR ★

JAPANESE →

Food holds a fervent, almost religious position in Japanese culture, and as such is always prepared with such devotion and precision that it is not strange to hear of chefs dedicating their lives to a single culinary art such as cooking sushi rice or folding soba noodles.

With that in mind, it is natural to presume that to attempt to make Japanese food would be a foolhardy pursuit as even if you could get your hands on the necessary equipment you would surely become unstuck at some point during preparation. However nothing could be further from the truth. Japanese food is now very well served by high street retailers. Seaweed, soy sauce, sushi rice and fresh noodles are easily found in many supermarkets and cooking procedures are very simple.

At its most basic level, Japanese food is incredibly easy to prepare. Much like other Asian cuisine, the Japanese use a few basic sauces to bring ingredients to life. Freshly steamed rice seasoned with a delicate balance of salt and vinegar is delicious on its own but reaches new heights when topped with fresh fish and dipped in soy sauce. What may initially seem complicated and intimidating is the very opposite. Just ensure you buy good quality ingredients and treat them with respect, and I can promise you that you will soon be a new devotee to Japanese cooking.

VEGETABLE TEMPURA

SERVES 4

Tempura is a wonderful batter that is both delicately thin, yet satisfyingly crunchy.
Even the briefest internet search will bring up hundreds of websites and whole essays
explaining the correct method of preparing the batter. Don't over-mix, keep it ice
cold, use chopsticks, stir clockwise... And so on. Whilst I respect the traditions of
Japanese food, my version rides roughshod over some of the stranger methods.
I stand proudly by it, as it is accessible, and most importantly easy. This batter can
be used on almost any ingredient, from butterflied prawns to chopped courgette.

PREP TIME: 20 MINS
COOKING TIME: 10 MINS

1 onion, finely diced
**1 carrot, cut into 4cm-
    long matchsticks**
**1 small potato, cut into
    4cm-long matchsticks**
**75g fine green beans,
    trimmed and sliced
    in half lengthways**
**about 1 litre sunflower
    or vegetable oil,
    for deep-frying**
75g self-raising flour
75g cornflour
1 tsp salt
200ml sparkling water
3 tbsp light soy sauce
1 tbsp rice wine vinegar
**1 red chilli, deseeded and
    finely sliced (optional)**
**salt and freshly ground
    black pepper**

Place the onion, carrot, potato and green beans in a large
bowl, season with salt and pepper and toss with your hands.

Heat the oil in a large, wide saucepan or deep fryer to 180°C.

Tip the self-raising flour, cornflour and salt into a large bowl.
Pour in the sparkling water and whisk slowly to bring all the
ingredients together into a smooth batter. Do not over-mix, it
is better to have a couple of lumps than to overwork the batter.

Mix together the soy sauce, vinegar and chilli to make the
dipping sauce. Leave to one side.

Tip the prepared vegetables into the bowl with the batter
and again, with your lightest touch, mix the vegetables so
that they become coated in the batter.

Using chopsticks, your fingers or a fork pick up a small
mound (about 2–3 heaped tablespoons) of the batter-coated
vegetables and carefully lower into the hot oil. The batter
should hold the vegetables, and the little pile will puff up and
bubble. Add a few more heaps to your hot oil, ensuring that
you don't overcrowd the pan. Fry the vegetable tempura for
about 4 minutes, by which time the batter should have turned
lightly golden and the vegetables will be just cooked through.

Keep the cooked tempura warm in the oven whilst you finish
frying the remainder. Serve with the simple dipping sauce.
You may never order prawn tempura again.

PRAWN *and* PORK GYOZA

MAKES 18

In the East, prawn and pork have been paired together for centuries.
Be it in wontons or in stir fries, the natural fattiness of the pork complements
and accentuates the sweetness of juicy prawns. I have opted for an elaborate
presentation method. If you find it too fiddly or you can't source prawns
with the tail on then simply mince the prawns with a knife and mix together
with the pork. You might find it tricky to source the wonton wrappers anywhere
other than in Asian supermarkets; my advice is that once you've found
them, stockpile them in your freezer.

PREP TIME: 30 MINS
COOKING TIME: 20 MINS

100g minced pork
2 cloves garlic, minced
2cm piece fresh ginger,
    peeled and grated
4 spring onions, trimmed
    and finely sliced
1 egg white
1 heaped tbsp cornflour
5 tbsp light soy sauce
1 tbsp sesame oil
18 gyoza wrappers
18 raw medium prawns,
    peeled apart from
    the tip of the tail
sunflower or vegetable oil,
    for frying
1 tbsp rice wine vinegar

Place the pork, garlic, ginger, spring onions, egg white,
cornflour, 2 tablespoons of the soy sauce and the sesame
oil in a bowl. Mix thoroughly to ensure all ingredients are
fully combined, then set this to one side.

I like to construct multiple gyoza at once, so I lay out four
wrappers in front of me at a time– this will quicken the
process. If you feel more comfortable tackling one at a time
then simply lay one wrapper in front of you. You will also
need a small bowl of water.

Spoon about half a tablespoon of the pork mixture into
the middle of the wrapper, flattening it down a little with
the back of the spoon. Next lay one of the prawns on top of
the mince with the head end in the middle and the tail tip
sticking out to one side. Dip your finger in the water and run
it all the way around the edge of the wrapper. Carefully pick
up the wrapper with the filling and press the edges together.
The prawn tail will protrude – this is good. Carefully pinch
the edges together all the way around so that you end up
with a sealed semi-circlular shape that has a prawn tail
sticking out from it (see picture overleaf). Repeat the

CONTINUED OVERLEAF

process with the remaining filling, prawns and wrappers. I promise you will improve and speed up.

When you have prepared all your gyoza and are ready to cook, fill a jug with water and place it next to the hob where you will be cooking. Pour about 2 tablespoons of oil into a large, non-stick frying pan for which you have a lid and place over a medium-high heat. When hot add some of the gyoza (it will most likely be necessary to cook them in at least two batches), and fry, without moving or turning for about 1 minute, or until they are crisp and golden.

Still without turning the gyoza, pour in about 3–4 tablespoons of water and immediately place the lid on the pan. Leave the gyoza to cook in the steam for 1 minute before lifting the lid and taking a peek. You need to cook the gyoza for about 3 minutes with water but if, when you take a peek you notice that there is no water left in the base of the frying pan, pour in a little more, but not too much – your aim is to finish the cooking process with no water left in the base of the pan.

After 3 minutes, remove the lid, and break one of the gyoza open to ensure that it is cooked through. If it is, then remove from the pan, and cook the rest of the gyoza in the same fashion.

When ready to serve, mix the remaining soy sauce with the rice wine vinegar and place in a shallow dish for dipping. Serve up your delicious gyoza.

VEGETABLE MISO SOUP

SERVES 2

Miso paste is a by-product of the fermentation process used to make soy sauce. In very basic terms it is the delicious gunk that is left behind in the pot when the soy sauce has been poured off. It is so very tasty because it is packed with natural glutamates that many of us know as 'umami'. If a dish contains umami your taste buds will find it irresistible. With that in mind, I have decided to put the moreish properties of miso to good use and have packed this enticing soup full of veggies.

PREP TIME: 5 MINS
COOKING TIME: 10 MINS

1 litre light chicken
    or vegetable stock
4 heaped tbsp brown
    miso paste
6 shiitake mushrooms,
    halved
150g tenderstem broccoli,
    halved lengthways
200g firm tofu, cut into
    2cm cubes
generous handful of
    baby leaf spinach
1 red chilli, deseeded
    and finely sliced
2 spring onions, finely sliced
black sesame seeds to
    garnish (optional)

Place the stock in a large saucepan and bring to the boil, then reduce the heat to a simmer. Dollop the miso paste into a bowl and add a couple of ladles of the warm stock to it. Use a spoon to stir the paste into the warm liquid until it has all dissolved. Pour this mixture back into the simmering stock and stir thoroughly to dissolve.

Add the mushrooms to the stock and allow to simmer for 2 minutes before adding the tenderstem broccoli and tofu. Allow the liquid to come back up to a simmer and cook for a further 2 minutes.

Divide the spinach between two bowls, and when ready to eat, ladle the simmering miso soup into the bowls directly on top of the spinach. Garnish your soup with the chilli, spring onions, and some black sesame seeds, if liked, before tucking in.

SMOKED MACKEREL and BEETROOT DONBURI

SERVES 2

A donburi is a lightly seasoned bowl of sticky rice topped with pretty much anything you like. Just to showcase the versatility of this dish, I have swayed towards the West for the topping in this version. Ingredients may be different, but the result is still delicious and incredibly healthy.

PREP TIME: 5 MINS
COOKING TIME: 20 MINS

1 batch of Seasoned Sushi
    Rice (see page 104)
3 smoked mackerel fillets,
    peeled
1 large cooked beetroot,
    cut into 5mm slices
1 small Granny Smith apple,
    peeled and chopped into
    matchsticks, or grated
small handful of
    rocket leaves
black or white sesame
    seeds, toasted, to serve

Divide the cooked sushi rice between two bowls.

Break the mackerel flesh into medium-sized flakes, discarding any bones that you come across, then divide the flakes between the bowls.

Arrange the beetroot discs on top of the rice next to the mackerel, then scatter the apple over the fish and beetroot.

Finish the dish with a scattering of rocket leaves and toasted sesame seeds.

BROWN RICE *and* EDAMAME SALAD

SERVES 2

Brown rice is full of health benefits but it also has a delicate, yet robust
nutty flavour which is far too often overlooked. I've used brown rice in this
recipe because the grains stand up to the strong flavours of ginger, vinegar
and radishes. Where white rice would only absorb the strong flavours
and become a muddled conduit, brown rice confidently carries them.
I suggest using brown rice any time you prepare a rice salad.

PREP TIME: 10 MINS
COOKING TIME: 20 MINS

5cm piece fresh ginger, peeled
2 tbsp mirin
2 tbsp rice wine vinegar
3 spring onions, trimmed
    and finely sliced
1 tsp sesame oil
400g cooked brown rice,
    cooled
200g edamame beans,
    frozen are perfect –
    simply defrost before use
7 radishes, trimmed and
    roughly chopped
¼ cucumber, peeled,
    deseeded and chopped into
    1cm dice
small handful of pea shoots
    or spinach

Place a clean J-cloth or a small square of muslin in front
of you on the worktop. Grate the ginger directly on to the
cloth. Gather up the sides and squeeze the ginger, ensuring
you catch as much of the juice as possible in a small bowl.
Discard the ginger pulp.

To the ginger juice add the mirin, rice wine vinegar,
spring onions and sesame oil. Stir the ingredients together
vigorously until they are well blended. Keep to one side.

Tip the cooled brown rice, edamame beans, radishes
and cucumber into a bowl. Add the dressing and mix
well with the other ingredients.

Divide the seasoned rice between two plates and top
with either pea shoots or spinach.

SEASONED SUSHI RICE

SERVES 4

When preparing rice for sushi, it is important to buy packets marked 'sushi rice'. Sushi rice grains are much shorter and plumper than either basmati or jasmine rice, and they have a distinctly different flavour. The method I describe below can be used to cook almost all varieties of rice; it is the salty and sour seasoning that transforms it into sushi rice.

PREP TIME: 10 MINS
COOKING TIME: 20 MINS

300g sushi rice
6 tbsp rice wine vinegar
2 tsp caster sugar
2 tsp fine salt

Place the rice in a saucepan for which you have a lid and cover with water. Leave the rice to soak for 20 minutes.

Drain the rice through a sieve, then run it under cold running water for a minute or so, running your fingers through the rice to remove excess starch. Ensure the rice is drained well and then tip it back into the saucepan. Pour in 450ml water, giving the pan a little shake to level the rice.

Place the saucepan over a high heat and when the liquid is vigorously boiling place the lid on top and reduce the heat to its minimum setting. Leave the rice to cook like this for 12 minutes – do not remove the lid. Turn the heat off, but leave the pan covered on the hob for a further 5 minutes; again, it is very important that you do not remove the lid.

Whilst the rice is resting tip the vinegar, sugar and salt into a small saucepan and heat gently. As the vinegar warms stir the ingredients until both the sugar and salt are fully dissolved, then remove from the heat.

When your rice has had its requisite resting time you can remove the lid. The liquid should have all been absorbed, and you should be greeted by perfectly cooked rice.

Pour the seasoning over the rice, then use a fork to rake the rice, mixing the seasoning through it. Leave the rice to soak up the seasoning for a further 5 minutes, before giving it all one last rake and a mix.

SALMON and AVOCADO TEMAKI (HAND ROLL)

MAKES 16 ROLLS

Perfecting the art of making sushi can take decades of devoted service, studying every nuance of the process. However if you are just looking to learn enough to sate your sushi craving then you can put together a very satisfying plate of sushi using the rice recipe opposite and the freshest fish you can find.

PREP TIME: 15 MINS
COOKING TIME: 20 MINS

1 x 500g piece salmon
   fillet, skinned
1 avocado, peeled and
   stoned
½ cucumber, sliced
   in half lengthways
   and deseeded
8 sheets nori seaweed,
   roughly 20 x 20cm
400g cooked Seasoned
   Sushi Rice
   (see page 104)
2 tbsp sesame seeds,
   toasted
wasabi, to serve
light soy sauce, to serve

It is a very good idea to prep all of your ingredients as follows before starting to make your hand roll.

Slice the salmon in half along the width. This should result in two quite thin but wide slabs of fish. Slice each piece of fish lengthways into 8 pieces. Place your 16 pieces of fish on a clean plate.

Slice the avocado in half lengthways, then slice each half into 8 wedges and again place on the plate.

Slice each cucumber half into eight long pieces on the diagonal. Place your 16 pieces of cucumber next to the avocado. You are now ready to make your hand rolls.

Slice one of the sheets of nori in half. Lay one half in front of you and spread a thin layer of rice over half of it. Scatter a few toasted sesame seeds on top of the rice. Lay a piece of salmon, a slice of avocado, and a slice of cucumber diagonally on to the rice with the tips of the ingredients pointing out of the seaweed (see picture overleaf).

Carefully pick up the seaweed in one hand, and tightly fold the bottom corner of the seaweed over the raw ingredients to create the cone shape. Wrap the excess seaweed around the cone, and fasten it together with a couple of grains of sticky rice.

Repeat the process with the remaining ingredients until you have 16 glorious temaki.

Serve with a good dollop of wasabi and lashings of soy sauce.

HONEY TOFU SALAD

SERVES 2

Tofu is undoubtedly good for us, packed to the gunnels with protein and virtually fat free; but it can also be a bit of an acquired taste with many regarding it as bland. But tofu can work brilliantly as a vehicle for other flavours and textures, so even if you don't think you like tofu have a go at this recipe and enjoy the feeling of virtue, which is sure to follow.

PREP TIME: 15 MINS
COOKING TIME: 0 MINS

1 tbsp clear honey
2 tbsp rice wine vinegar
2 tsp sesame oil
1 tbsp light soy sauce
2 carrots, grated
small handful of
    beansprouts, washed
2 spring onions, trimmed
    and sliced into 1cm pieces
1 red pepper, deseeded
    and thinly sliced
1 clove garlic, very
    finely chopped
1 x 250g block of silken tofu
handful of pea shoots
    or baby spinach
black sesame seeds,
    to serve (optional)

To make the dressing, pour the honey, rice wine vinegar, sesame oil and soy sauce into a bowl. Whisk the ingredients together until fully combined.

Place the carrots, beansprouts, spring onions, red pepper and garlic into a bowl. Mix well with a spoon, or with your hands (my perferred method). Pour half of the dressing over the salad, and mix again to ensure all the ingredients are well coated.

Divide the salad mixture between two plates. Remove the tofu from its packaging and depending on how soft it is either slice into cubes or spoon it on to the salad.

Finally, top the salad with pea shoots and a scattering of black sesame seeds, if liked. Finish by spooning over the remaining dressing.

CHICKEN YAKI UDON

SERVES 4

By using ready-to-wok udon noodles this meal becomes lightning fast to cook, so whilst others are still perusing the menu, you can be tucking in to a steaming bowl of noodles. Don't feel bound to the recipe; the meat and vegetables can be adapted to whatever you have in the fridge.

PREP TIME: 10 MINS
COOKING TIME: 9 MINS

4 skinless, boneless
   chicken thighs, cut
   into 1cm-thick slices
1 heaped tablespoon
   cornflour
4 tbsp light soy sauce
2 tbsp sunflower or
   vegetable oil, for frying
4 cloves garlic, finely diced
6 spring onions, trimmed
   and sliced 1cm thick
1 red pepper, deseeded
   and cut into 5mm slices
100g green beans, trimmed
500g fresh udon noodles,
   altenatively use 200g
   dried noodles,cooking
   according to packet
2 tsp fish sauce
2 tsp sesame oil
salt and freshly ground
   black pepper

Place the chicken pieces into a bowl, and sprinkle over the cornflour, along with a little salt and pepper. Pour over 2 tablespoons of the soy sauce, and using a spoon mix the ingredients together as well as you can. Leave the chicken to sit for 10 minutes.

When ready to cook, heat the oil in a large frying pan or wok over a high heat. When hot tip in the chicken, and fry for 2–3 minutes, separating the pieces with a wooden spoon. Add the garlic and spring onions and continue to fry, stirring intermittently, for a further 2 minutes.

Add the red pepper and green beans, again frying and stirring over a high heat for a further minute.

Add the noodles and use a combination of utensils (I like to use two wooden spoons) to mix them into the other ingredients. Continue to fry and stir for 1 minute.

Remove the pan from the hob and pour in the fish sauce, remaining soy sauce and sesame oil. Give the whole lot one last stir to mix in the seasonings before divvying the noodles up between plates. A perfect midweek dinner, ready in minutes.

CHICKEN KATSU

SERVES 2

Chicken breast coated in crunchy breadcrumbs, fried until crisp
on the outside but beautifully moist inside, then topped with a homely
curry sauce – this one of the most irresistible Japanese dishes.

PREP TIME: 15 MINS
COOKING TIME: 20 MINS

3 tbsp vegetable oil
1 small onion, diced
**1 stick celery, trimmed
and diced**
**1 clove garlic,
finely chopped**
**2cm piece fresh ginger,
peeled and finely
chopped**
**1 small apple, peeled,
cored and roughly diced**
1 tbsp mild curry powder
**300ml chicken or
vegetable stock**
50g flour
1 egg
75g fresh breadcrumbs
2 chicken breasts
**freshly cooked rice,
to serve**
**Pickled Cucumbers
(see page 44), to serve
(optional)**

Heat 1 tablespoon of the oil in a medium saucepan over a
medium-high heat. When hot tip in the onion and fry, stirring
regularly, for about 5 minutes until the onion has softened but
remains colourless. Add the celery, garlic, ginger, apple and curry
powder. Fry the ingredients for 1 minute, stirring regularly.

Pour in the stock and bring to the boil. Leave the sauce
to simmer gently for about 20 minutes by which time the
ingredients should have become incredibly soft. The cooking
ingredients should always be covered by stock; if they are
not, simply add a little extra.

Purée the sauce using either a jug blender, stick blender or
mouli, until very smooth. Keep the sauce warm whilst you
cook your chicken.

Tip the flour on to a plate, and crack the egg into a wide bowl
and whisk it up. Spread your breadcrumbs over a plate. Season
a chicken breast liberally with salt and pepper before dropping
it into the flour, patting off any of the excess, then slicking it
with the beaten egg and finally rolling it in the breadcrumbs.
Repeat the process with the second breast.

Heat the remaining 2 tablespoons of oil in a large frying pan
over a medium-high heat. When hot, gently lower in the breaded
chicken. Fry the breasts for about 3 minutes on each side until
the breadcrumbs turn dark golden and the chicken is fully
cooked through. If you are unsure about the chicken being
cooked, cut into the thickest part of the breast with a sharp
knife and check all the flesh has turned from pink to white.

Slice up the fried chicken, and serve alongside rice, pickled
cucumbers and lashings of the curry sauce.

TERIYAKI RIBEYE

SERVES 2

I'm quite sure that the word 'teriyaki' should be translated into English as 'eat me, I'm delicious', because it seems that anything basted with this lustrous marinade becomes irresistible. Try to use slightly fatty ribeye steak for this recipe, simply because it's a satisfying cut of meat that acts as the perfect vehicle for the moreish marinade. Or try chicken thighs for a change; the cooking and marinating times are identical.

PREP TIME: 10 MINS,
PLUS 1 HOUR MARINATING TIME
COOKING TIME: 8 MINS
FOR MEDIUM-RARE

100ml light soy sauce
50ml mirin
2 tbsp clear honey
1 clove garlic, crushed
2cm piece fresh ginger,
**   peeled and grated**
1 x 400g ribeye steak
cooked rice, cabbage
**   and salad, to serve**

Pour the soy sauce, mirin and honey into a bowl. Add the garlic and ginger. Mix well with a spoon until well combined.

Place the steak in a bowl, and pour over the marinade. Swish the meat about in the dish to ensure an even coating. Marinate the meat for a minimum of 1 hour but preferably overnight. If leaving to marinate for a long time ensure that you cover and refrigerate the meat but also ensure that you remove the meat from the fridge in time for it to return to room temperature before cooking.

When ready to cook, heat a griddle pan over a high heat; if you don't have a griddle use a heavy-based frying pan. Pick up the steak, draining it of excess marinade, and place directly on to the hot pan. Fry on each side for about 4 minutes for medium-rare meat. Whilst the steak is cooking use a pastry brush to paint the meat with the remaining marinade. Remove the steak to a plate and leave to rest in a warm place for 5 minutes. This cooking method will result in a medium-rare steak which I suggest is perfect. If you prefer your steak more or less cooked then adjust your cooking time – just ensure you allow the steak a generous amount of time to rest.

Serve the steak, either whole, or sliced into strips with rice, cabbage and a small salad.

CHAPTER
FIVE
ITALIAN

To think that a humble recipe from the backstreets of Naples has become one of the world's most ordered takeaways is quite mindboggling. From the high rises of New York to roadside shacks in Vietnam you can pretty much find a pizza anywhere in the world, with almost any topping your mind can conjure.

And where pizza has travelled, arancini, lasagne and spaghetti have followed. The world has embraced and adopted Italian food as its own. Yet many takeaways seem to find it very easy to ruin the fresh flavours of the quality ingredients on which Italian cuisine is based. Too often pizza arrives on a flabby base of chewy dough, topped with a mass of melted cheese drenched in indigestible grease. This may be satisfying in the short term, but ultimately it's too much for your stomach and body to process.

It's time to claim Italian food back and cook our own fresh, satisfying versions.

POLENTA CHIPS

SERVES 4

These polenta chips are pan-fried as opposed to deep-fried like their
potato counterparts. Not only does this make them better for you, it makes
them a lot less hassle to prepare. In fact, I would go as far as saying that
for subtle dishes such as fish or salads, the Parmesan-bolstered flavour
makes these a better accompaniment than potato chips.

PREP TIME: 10 MINS
COOKING TIME: 15 MINS,
PLUS ABOUT 1 HOUR TO SET

olive oil, for greasing
    and frying
300g quick-cook polenta
90g Parmesan, grated
large knob of butter
½ bunch of sage, leaves
    only, finely chopped
salt and freshly ground
    black pepper
Tomato Sauce (see page 141),
    to serve

Take a shallow tray (it doesn't have to be a cooking one),
roughly 30 x 30cm, and drizzle a little olive oil over it. Smear
the oil all over the tray. Roll out a piece of cling film big enough
to cover the tray with a little overhang. Lay the cling film in
the tray and push it into the corners; the olive oil will help
the film stick to the tray. Leave to one side.

Cook the polenta according to the packet instructions
and when you are happy that it is ready, remove from the
heat and immediately add the Parmesan, butter and chopped
sage. Stir the mixture again, adding a generous amount
of both salt and pepper.

Pour and scrape the polenta into the lined tray. You are
aiming for a layer about 2cm deep. Use a wet spoon or spatula
to smooth out the surface. Leave the polenta uncovered to
cool to room temperature. If you are preparing the day before
then when the polenta is at room temperature, cover and place
in the fridge until ready to serve.

When you are ready to serve the polenta chips, flip the tray
on to your chopping board. The polenta should have cooled
into a solid slab from which you are able to peel the cling film.

Use a sharp knife to portion the polenta into wedge sized chips.
Drizzle the chips with a little olive oil and either fry them
in a hot, dry frying pan or slick with olive oil and brown under
a hot grill for 1 minute on each side. The Tomato Sauce is
delicious served alongside.

TOMATO *and* MOZZARELLA BRUSCHETTA

SERVES 2

Bruschetta is essentially a slice of toasted bread. Traditionally it was used as a way for producers to showcase their olive oils – they drizzled the oil over toasted bread and potential customers were able to taste and judge its quality. Bruschetta has since evolved, and although the principle of the toasted bread still exists, where there was once only olive oil now sit any number of ingredient combinations your creativity can muster, transforming this old sales technique into a perfect lunch or light dinner.

PREP TIME: 15 MINS
COOKING TIME: 10 MINS

10 cherry tomatoes,
    preferably on the vine
good quality olive oil,
    for drizzling
2 thick slices of sourdough
    or other good quality
    rustic bread
1 clove garlic, peeled
125g ball of mozzarella
½ bunch of basil, leaves only
drizzle of balsamic vinegar
salt and freshly ground
    black pepper
walnut halves, roughly
    chopped, to serve
    (optional)

Preheat your oven to 190°C/fan 180°C/375°F/gas mark 5 and the grill to maximum.

Place the cherry tomatoes on a roasting tray, drizzle with a little olive oil and season with salt and pepper. Roast the tomatoes in the oven for 8–10 minutes. The tomatoes are ready when the skin bursts and they turn soft but still hold their shape. It is worth noting that the riper the tomatoes the less time they will take to cook.

Drizzle the slices of sourdough bread with a few generous glugs of olive oil and place them under the grill. Grill for about 2 minutes each side; you are aiming for the bread to be deep golden all over.

When the bread is toasted, remove from the grill and immediately rub with the garlic clove. The coarse surface of the bread acts as a natural grater, picking up the delicious flavour of the garlic. Be careful at this point, as you may suddenly realise you have grated half a clove on to each slice of toasted bread.

When you are ready to serve, place the toasted bread slices on two plates, tear the mozzarella into large chunks and place on the bread before carefully laying the roasted tomatoes on top. Scatter with basil leaves and then finish with a drizzle of balsamic vinegar and the walnut pieces, if using.

ARANCINI
(FRIED RICE BALLS)

MAKES 18

These little balls carry a flawless combination of textures. A crisp breadcrumb shell gives way to the creamy, smooth texture of risotto – what else could your mouth possibly want or need? There are endless possibilities with arancini, but I think these classic mozzarella-stuffed balls are best because of the instant comfort that comes from melted cheese.

PREP TIME: 40 MINS
COOKING TIME: 45 MINS

knob of butter
generous splash of olive oil
2 banana shallots,
    finely diced
1 clove garlic, finely chopped
200g risotto rice
3 tbsp white wine vinegar
150ml white wine
750ml hot vegetable stock
40g Parmesan, grated
½ bunch of parsley,
    finely chopped
150g firm mozzarella
2 eggs
100g plain flour
100g fresh breadcrumbs
12 sage leaves,
    finely chopped
about 500ml vegetable oil,
    for shallow-frying
salt and freshly ground
    black pepper
Tomato Sauce (see page 141),
    to serve

Heat the butter and olive oil in a medium saucepan over a medium-high heat. When the butter has melted and is bubbling in the oil add the shallots and cook, stirring regularly, for 2 minutes before adding the garlic and continuing to stir and fry for a further minute.

Add the rice and immediately stir to coat it with the combination of hot butter and oil. Fry the rice with the other ingredients, stirring almost constantly, for 2 minutes.

Pour in the white wine vinegar and let it bubble away to almost nothing. Pour in the white wine, and again let the wine evaporate until it has virtually disappeared.

Pour in about a quarter of the vegetable stock, stirring the rice almost constantly, and let the rice absorb the stock so that it reduces and the pan seems to be running dry, then add the next quarter and continue the process of stirring and cooking. Repeat until all the stock is used up and the rice has developed its trademark creamy texture. The process should take about 25–30 minutes, at which point the rice will be al dente.

Remove the cooked risotto from the heat, stir in the Parmesan and parsley, then tip the risotto into a bowl and leave, uncovered, to cool to room temperature.

Whilst the risotto is cooling, chop the mozzarella into twelve 1.5cm cubes and place in the fridge. Crack the

CONTINUED OVERLEAF

eggs into a bowl and beat them thoroughly. Tip the flour into another bowl and season generously with salt and pepper, and finally tip the breadcrumbs on to a third plate and mix with the sage.

When the risotto has cooled enough to handle, lightly wet your hands, and scoop out a small amount of the risotto – ultimately you are aiming to divide this mixture into 18 to form roughly equal-sized arancini. Pick up one of the mozzarella cubes and gently squeeze the risotto around the cheese. When you are happy with your work place the ball on to a piece of baking parchment and repeat the process with the remaining risotto and mozzarella.

Taking one ball at a time roll it in flour, coat in beaten egg and finally roll in the herby crumbs. Repeat with the rest of the balls.

Heat roughly 2cm of vegetable oil in a wide, high-sided frying pan or saucepan. You are aiming for it to reach about 170°C. To test if the temperature of the oil is correct drop in some of the breadcrumbs – they should take about 30 seconds to turn a deep golden colour. Carefully lower a few of the crumbed balls into the hot oil, the oil should reach about half way up the sides of the balls. Fry the balls for about 1 minute, before turning and frying for a further minute.

Remove the arancini to a piece of kitchen paper to drain any excess oil, and keep them warm in a low oven whilst you cook the remaining balls.

Serve the arancini with a generous spoonful of the tomato sauce and get busy thinking up your own perfect flavour combinations.

SPAGHETTI BOLOGNESE

SERVES 4

For many people Bolognese, and more specifically their mum's spaghetti Bolognese, would make it on to the menu of their 'last supper', such is the strength of feeling towards this Italian classic. This recipe is full of vegetables, which transforms it into the perfect all-in-one meal. For something a little different try drizzling just a little balsamic vinegar on top of your plated Bolognese – the sour vinegary tang adds another dimension to the classic. I would suggest doubling up this recipe and cooking it once a month, portioning it and then freezing it; that way you know you will always have a hearty meal close to hand.

PREP TIME: 30 MINS
COOKING TIME: ABOUT 2 HOURS

**4 tbsp olive oil, plus
a little extra to drizzle
1 large onion, diced
1 large carrot, cut into
    1cm cubes
3 sticks celery, cut into
    1cm cubes
3 cloves garlic, finely sliced
1 fresh bay leaf
2 sprigs of fresh thyme
1 heaped tbsp tomato purée
1 large glass of red wine
1 x 400g tin chopped
    tomatoes
500ml beef stock
1kg minced beef
350g dried or fresh spaghetti
salt and freshly ground
    black pepper
Parmesan, to serve
chopped parsley, to serve**

Heat 2 tablespoons of the olive oil in a large saucepan or ovenproof pan over a medium-high heat. When hot add the onion, and let it fry, stirring regularly for 2 minutes before adding the carrot, celery and garlic. Fry the vegetables, stirring regularly for 5 minutes before adding the bay leaf and thyme, then continue to fry for a further minute.

Add the tomato purée to the frying vegetables and stir to incorporate. Fry the mixture, stirring almost constantly for 1 minute before increasing the heat to maximum and pouring in the red wine. Bring the wine up to the boil and let it bubble until it has reduced by half. Add the tomatoes and the stock along with a generous amount of salt and pepper. Bring the mixture up to the boil, then reduce the heat and leave to simmer whilst you prepare the meat.

Heat 1 tablespoon of the olive oil in a frying pan over a high heat. When hot add half the minced beef. Use a wooden spoon to break up the pieces of beef as it fries. Fry the beef for 2–3 minutes over the high heat until some of the pieces of meat have browned and you have broken it up into small pieces; when this has happened tip the cooked mince into the simmering sauce. Repeat the process with the last tablespoon of olive oil and the remaining beef. When you

CONTINUED OVERLEAF

tip the meat into the pan ensure you scrape as much of the residue and liquid from the frying pan into the saucepan.

Bring the Bolognese to the boil, then reduce the heat to a simmer and cook for 1½ hours. Keep an eye on the Bolognese, adding a little stock to ensure the pan doesn't cook dry. After this time the Bolognese should have cooked into a thick sauce and the meat should be meltingly tender.

When you are almost at the end of the cooking time, cook the spaghetti according to the packet instructions in generously salted water. I always think it is worth testing the pasta about 2 minutes earlier than the packet suggests to ensure there is still a little bite left in it. When you are happy with the pasta, drain in a colander and then drizzle with a little olive oil and season with salt and pepper.

Tip the cooked spaghetti into the Bolognese, add grated Parmesan and a sprinkling of chopped parsley. Give the pan one last stir before serving up.

PASTA FUNGHI

Ingredients that might previously have been considered too exotic to be stocked in supermarkets are now readily available, and as shoppers, we are infinitely more savvy, recognising our rigatoni from our ravioli and our portabello from our porcini. This recipe takes advantage of the fresh pasta and dried porcini mushrooms we can now source easily, and uses them to make something simple into something truly delicious.

PREP TIME: 15 MINS
COOKING TIME: 20 MINS,
PLUS 10 MINS SOAKING TIME

50g dried porcini
   mushrooms
2 tbsp light olive oil
200g chestnut mushrooms,
   brushed clean and
   chopped in half
2 cloves garlic, peeled
   and finely sliced
3 sprigs of thyme
400g fresh or dried
   tagliatelle
100ml double cream
juice of ½ lemon
salt and freshly ground
   black pepper
¼ bunch of parsley,
   finely chopped, to serve
Parmesan, to serve

Place the dried porcini in a small bowl and cover with warm water. Leave to stand for 10 minutes. After 10 minutes drain the mushrooms, being sure to keep hold of the liquid. Roughly chop the mushrooms.

Heat the oil in a medium frying pan over a medium heat. When hot, add the chestnut mushrooms and fry for a couple of minutes before adding the rehydrated porcini. Liquid will be released from the porcini so just continue to cook them and the liquid will be absorbed by the chestnut mushrooms.

Add the garlic and thyme and continue to cook for about 10 minutes over the medium heat. As the mushrooms are cooking add a few tablespoons of the porcini liquid, leaving the mushrooms time to absorb the liquid.

Cook the tagliatelle according to the packet instructions, but before you drain the pasta save a mugful of the cloudy cooking liquid.

By the time the pasta is cooked the mushrooms should have had their requisite cooking time. Add the cream to the mushrooms along with the lemon juice and a pinch of salt and pepper. Stir to mix.

Tip the cooked tagliatelle into the pan of mushroom sauce, and add about 6 tablespoons of the cooking liquid to loosen the sauce to the consistency of single cream. Cook the sauce and the pasta together in the pan for 2 minutes before sprinkling with the parsley and a grating of Parmesan. Serve up your pasta in the middle of the table and let the masses pile in.

SPINACH and RICOTTA CANNELLONI

SERVES 4

Even the most ardent carnivore will forget about meat for at least the time it takes them to finish their plateful of this hearty pasta dish. The flavour combination of the salty cheeses and garlicky spinach more than makes up for the lack of meat.

PREP TIME: 45 MINS
COOKING TIME: 1 HOUR

50g butter
1 fresh bay leaf
50g plain flour
400ml milk
90g Parmesan, grated
2 tbsp olive oil
2 cloves garlic, finely sliced
250g baby leaf spinach
250g ricotta
grated zest of ½ lemon
fresh nutmeg
1 x 400g tin chopped tomatoes
1 bunch of basil, leaves only
1 ball of mozzarella, drained
8 large, dried cannelloni tubes
salt and freshly ground
    black pepper

Preheat your oven to 190°C/fan 180°C/375°F/gas mark 5.

Melt the butter in a saucepan over a medium heat and add the bay leaf. Tip in the flour and quickly stir to mix it into the butter. Cook the mixture, stirring constantly for 1 minute, then take the saucepan off the heat. Pour in a few glugs of the milk and stir to combine with the butter and flour mix – it might turn claggy, don't worry.

Pour in some more milk and again stir to combine. Place the saucepan back on a medium-high heat and add the remaining milk. Bring the milk to the boil whilst stirring almost constantly. This should result in a smooth white sauce. Remove the bay leaf and stir in half of the Parmesan. Leave your cheese sauce to one side.

Heat the olive oil in a large frying pan over a medium-high heat. When the oil is hot add the garlic and fry for 30 seconds, stirring almost constantly. Tip in the spinach and stir until the leaves are completely wilted. Transfer the cooked spinach to a colander, and apply a little pressure to squeeze out the excess liquid, then place in a bowl.

Crumble the ricotta over the spinach; I find scratching the cheese from the tub with a fork proves very effective. Add the lemon zest along with a generous grating of nutmeg. Season with plenty of salt and pepper and mix until well combined.

CONTINUED OVERLEAF

Tip the tinned tomatoes into the base of a 30x15cm ovenproof dish, season with a little salt and pepper. Scatter over a few basil leaves. Take one of the mozzarella balls and tear it up into chunks, dropping the pieces into the tomatoes.

Take a cannelloni tube and using a combination of teaspoon and your fingers, stuff it with the spinach and ricotta mixture. Ensure you fully fill the tube, even if the mixture hangs out of the ends. Repeat with all the tubes, and embed them in the tomato mixture in a single layer.

Spoon the cheese sauce over the top of the cannelloni. Don't worry too much about even coverage or being very neat, the pieces of pasta that aren't covered will turn satisfyingly crisp later on. Tear the remaining mozzarella ball into large chunks, and dot all over the dish. Your cannelloni can be covered and placed in the fridge at this point, and can be cooked up to two days later. Just ensure you remove the dish from the fridge a minimum of 1 hour before you place in the oven to allow it to come to room temperature.

If you are ready to eat then place the dish in the oven, and bake for about 35–45 minutes, until the sauce is bubbling and the pasta cooked through. If you are worried that the sauce is burning before the pasta is cooked then just cover the dish with tin foil, but you should be fine. Take your steaming dish of deliciousness to the table.

PASTA CARBONARA

SERVES 2

This popular Italian creation is so often short of the mark. A dish that is supposed to be simple, light and delicately creamy is all too commonly hit with the stodgy stick and becomes a heaving mess of bacon, mushrooms and white sauce. Granted, on a dark wintery night the heavyweight version can provide a certain comfort, but for any other situation or time of year the following recipe will put a spring in your step.

PREP TIME: 10 MINS
COOKING TIME: 15 MINS

2 eggs
45g Parmesan, grated
175g dried spaghetti
or linguine
large knob of butter
60g pancetta, chopped
into small cubes
¼ bunch of parsley,
finely chopped
salt and freshly ground
black pepper

Bring a large pan of salted water to the boil.

Meanwhile, crack the eggs into a bowl and add the Parmesan along with a generous pinch of black pepper. Beat the ingredients together. When the water has come to the boil drop in the pasta and cook according to the packet instructions.

Melt the butter in a large frying pan over a medium-high heat. When it is bubbling, add the pancetta and fry, stirring regularly for about 5 minutes by which time the pieces will be cooked and lightly golden. Take the frying pan off the heat.

Before draining the pasta save a mugful of the starchy cooking water. Drain the pasta through a colander, then immediately tip it into the frying pan with the cooked pancetta, and place the pan over a low heat. Mix well.

Pour half of the mug of water into the egg mixture and stir immediately with a fork. Pour the mixture into the pan with the pasta and pancetta. Using a combination of utensils (I find a pair of tongs and a fork works well) fold the spaghetti through the other ingredients. As you mix the sauce ingredients will emulsify and develop into a velvety sauce. Don't let the ingredients boil. Add a little extra starchy water if you feel the sauce is too thick – you are aiming for a consistency similar to single cream.

Divide the saucy spaghetti between two plates, sprinkle with the parsley and serve.

ROAST TOMATO and PESTO RISOTTO

SERVES 4

There is no secret to a good risotto, the key to achieving the luxuriously creamy texture is down to constant stirring, which draws the starch from the rice. Never let anybody tell you that your risotto is over- or under-cooked. In my opinion the correct texture for the rice is the one that you like, be it tooth-denting hardness, or baby food-like softness. This recipe gives directions on how to make a fresh pesto to stir through your risotto, which elevates the dish in flavour and appearance, but if you're making the dish with limited time then just use 4 tablespoons of ready-made pesto.

PREP TIME: 15 MINS
COOKING TIME: 45 MINS

3 large cloves garlic
large knob of butter
olive oil, for drizzling
3 banana shallots,
    finely diced
300g risotto rice
150ml white wine
800ml hot vegetable stock
16 cherry tomatoes,
    preferably still on
    the vine
salt and freshly ground
    black pepper

For the pesto
2 bunches of basil,
    thick stalks removed
50g Parmesan, grated
75ml olive oil, plus a
    little extra for frying
    and roasting
2 tbsp toasted pine nuts

Preheat your oven to 190°C/fan 180°C/375°F/gas mark 5.

Wrap the garlic cloves tightly in foil, place on a small tray and slide into the oven. Roast for 20 minutes.

If making fresh pesto, place the basil, Parmesan, olive oil and pine nuts in a food processor along with a generous pinch of both salt and pepper. Blitz the ingredients until smooth, then leave to one side.

Place the butter in a large saucepan along with a drizzle of olive oil. Heat the ingredients over a medium-high heat. When the butter is bubbling, add the shallots and fry, stirring regularly, for 3–4 minutes by which time the shallots will have softened.

Tip in the rice, and stir to slick with the oil and butter. Fry the rice for 1 minute, stirring almost constantly. The direct heat 'cracks' the grains which helps the release of starch and in turn gives the risotto its creamy texture. Pour in the wine and allow it to bubble down to less than half its original volume.

Pour in roughly a quarter of the stock, and stir whilst it bubbles up. Stir the risotto fairly constantly until the rice

CONTINUED OVERLEAF

ROAST TOMATO AND
PESTO RISOTTO
CONTINUED

has absorbed almost all of the liquid without the pan cooking dry. When there is very little liquid left add more stock, and continue the process of stirring. Continue adding stock and stirring for about 35 minutes, by which time all the stock should have been absorbed, the rice will have cooked to a pleasing texture, and the sauce thickened.

When your garlic has only 10 minutes left to roast (roughly as you add your final amount of stock to the risotto), remove the tray from the oven and add the cherry tomatoes. Drizzle with a little olive oil and season with salt and pepper. Slide the tray back into the oven, and roast the tomatoes for about 10 minutes, by which time they will have softened but will still retain their shape.

When you are happy with the consistency of your risotto remove it from the heat and add the pesto. Beat it in with a spoon; the melting Parmesan will add creaminess to the sauce. Taste your risotto, and adjust the seasoning as you wish.

Remove the roasted garlic and tomatoes from the oven. Unwrap the garlic, pinch the ends, and squeeze the soft flesh from the skin straight into your risotto. Mix the roasted garlic into the risotto. Serve the risotto topped with the roasted tomatoes.

PIZZA

SERVES 4

At its best pizza is a wondrously simple combination of soft dough with a crispy base and a sparse scattering of choice toppings. No one component overpowers any other; it is a beautiful example of synergetic cooking. At its worst pizza has become a monstrosity of greasy cheese and meat toppings on a base not too dissimilar to styrofoam. Bad pizza is the epitome of terrible takeaway food, loaded with fats, sugars and salts no body needs. I implore you to try my homemade version just once, and I assure you the pizza menu will soon find its place in the dusty gap behind the fridge.

BASIC DOUGH

MAKES ENOUGH FOR 4 PIZZAS

This recipe is incredibly simple and forms the base of all the pizza recipes in this chapter. It includes '00' flour which is widely available, but if you really can't find it then use strong bread flour, although you may need to use a little more or reduce the amount of liquid. Regard the following few pages as the building blocks to a better pizza experience. Do not feel the need to rush through the recipes cooking them all at once; take your time and enjoy the process. By simply starting with the basic dough and tomato sauce I promise you that you will not only realise what real pizza should taste like, but the connection you feel with your final dish will give you the impetus to try other recipes.

PREP TIME: 20 MINS,
PLUS PROVING TIME

12g fast-action yeast
2 tsp caster sugar
300ml lukewarm water
30ml good-quality olive oil,
  plus a little extra for
  greasing
500g '00' flour, plus a
  little extra for dusting
8g salt

Tip the yeast and sugar into a jug and pour over the warm water, using a spoon to mix thoroughly. Pour in the olive oil and give the mixture one final stir.

Tip the flour into a large bowl and add the salt.

Pour the yeast mixture into the flour, and begin to mix the ingredients together with a wooden spoon. When you can't mix with the spoon anymore tip the ingredients on to a

CONTINUED OVERLEAF

clean surface and begin to knead it with your hands. You will need to knead the dough for 5 minutes by which time it should be satisfyingly pliable and have a lustrous sheen.

Lightly oil a clean bowl, form the dough into a ball and place in the bowl. Cover with a greased piece of cling film, and leave to rise in a warm place for a minimum of 1½ hours. The pizza recipes (see pages 142–151) will pick up the dough from this point on.

DOUGH IDEAS

Make your own dough balls by rolling up any leftover pieces of dough and baking them alongside your pizzas.

If you don't use all of your dough in one go then either fry for 2 minutes each side in a lightly oiled frying pan over a medium-high heat and use as flatbreads, or roll the dough out, bake, leave to cool and then freeze. The bases can be topped later and cooked from frozen.

Make amazing garlic bread by pushing the dough into a baking tray, drizzling with olive oil, sprinkling with rosemary and chopped garlic and baking in an oven preheated to 220°C/210°C fan/425°F/gas mark 7 for 12–15 minutes.

TOMATO SAUCE

SERVES 2

If you are pushed for time and just need a quick fix, spooning shop-bought passata on to a pizza base will do the trick. However, if and when you do have a few spare minutes, this tomato sauce is well worth making. It's so easy to prepare, and once it's cooking can happily bubble away whilst your pizza dough is proving. Double up the recipe and freeze half for future pizza evenings, or defrost and use as the base for a simple bowl of pasta and sauce.

PREP TIME: 10 MINS
COOKING TIME: 45 MINS

2 tbsp olive oil
1 red onion, finely diced
1 clove garlic, finely sliced
1 tbsp tomato purée
1 tbsp balsamic vinegar
1 x 400g tin chopped
    tomatoes
1 tsp sugar
salt and freshly ground
    black pepper

Heat the oil in a saucepan over a medium-high heat. When hot add the onion and fry, stirring regularly, for 4 minutes, by which time the onion will have softened and taken on a little colour. Add the garlic, and continue to stir and fry for a further minute.

Add the tomato purée and mix thoroughly. Fry the mixture for 1 minute, stirring almost constantly to stop the purée from burning. Pour in the vinegar and let it bubble away to almost nothing before tipping in the tin of tomatoes.

Pour in enough water to fill the emptied tomato tin half way and use the water to swill the remaining tomato from the tin before adding it to the bubbling sauce. Add the sugar along with a generous amount of both salt and pepper and stir. Bring the sauce to the boil before reducing the heat to a simmer and cooking for about 30 minutes, stirring occasionally. The sauce will have thickened to a satisfying consistency. You can use the sauce like this or you can blitz it until smooth to make a slightly more refined sauce.

MARGHERITA PIZZA

MAKES 4 PIZZAS

If ever there were a hall of fame for food the margherita pizza would be a certainty for inclusion. Supposedly developed with the colours of the Italian flag in mind, the toppings of mozzarella, basil and tomatoes are as close to perfection as pizza makers have managed to achieve. Whilst everybody is trying to crowbar on increasingly elaborate toppings the pizza margherita stands up for culinary simplicity. Bellissima!

PREP TIME: 30 MINS,
PLUS PROVING TIME
COOKING TIME: 40 MINS

flour, for dusting
1 batch of Basic Dough
   (see page 139)
about 2 tablespoons polenta,
   for dusting
½ batch of Tomato Sauce
   (see page 141), at room
   temperature or cooler
2–3 balls of mozzarella,
   depending on how cheesy
   you like your pizza
1 bunch of basil, leaves only
salt and freshy ground
   black pepper
olive oil, for drizzling

Preheat your oven to 240°C/230°C fan/475°F/gas mark 9. Place a thick, flat baking tray in the oven and leave it to heat for at least 20 minutes.

Generously dust a clean surface with flour. Tip your risen dough out on to the floured surface, and knock the air out by kneading it for a couple of minutes. Divide the dough into four.

Take one portion of the dough and roll it out to a diameter of about 30cm, roughly the thickness of a pound coin. Do not be too concerned about making a perfect circle; I very rarely do, and as long as the dough is roughly the same thickness all over it won't make a difference to the taste or texture.

When you are happy with the shape dust a tray or chopping board with the polenta. Carefully lay the rolled dough out on the polenta, gently pushing the dough back into shape with your fingers.

Spoon a couple of tablespoons of the tomato sauce on to the pizza base, and spread it all over using the back of the spoon, leaving a 1cm border around the edge. Tear chunks of the mozzarella and dot them all over the tomato, then scatter over some of the basil leaves and season with salt and pepper.

CONTINUED OVERLEAF

The next bit needs to be done as quickly as you are able. Ensure that the pizza is free to move around on the polenta-dusted surface. When you're happy the pizza will slide, quickly remove the preheated tray from the oven and slip the prepared pizza straight on to it.

Place the tray back in the oven and bake for 12 minutes, by which time the cheese will have melted, and the dough will have bubbled up a little on top and turned crisp on the base.

At this point you can start preparing your next pizza by rolling out a second ball of dough on a polenta dusted surface, and topping with tomato sauce and mozzarella.

When baked, remove the pizza from the oven and slide it on to a board. Slip your next pizza in to the oven to keep the pizza conveyor belt running. You can either top your cooked pizza with more basil leaves and a drizzle of olive oil and serve immediately, or wait until the rest of the pizzas are made and serve all at once.

MUSHROOM, SPINACH and TALEGGIO PIZZA BIANCO

MAKES 4 PIZZAS

This style of pizza is not as well known outside of Italy as its more popular tomato-topped cousin, nonetheless it is just as delicious, and I think suits bold ingredients like mushrooms and strong cheese better than the classic pizza. It's also a very convenient recipe to pull out when you've forgotten to pick up any tinned tomatoes!

PREP TIME: 35 MINS,
PLUS PROVING TIME
COOKING TIME: 15 MINS

2 tbsp olive oil, plus extra
    for drizzling
4 large Portobello
    mushrooms, brushed clean
    and cut into 1cm slices
250g baby leaf spinach
flour, for dusting
1 batch of Basic Dough
    (see page 139)
about 2 tablespoons polenta,
    for dusting
200g Taleggio cheese, cut
    into chunks
salt and freshly ground
    black pepper
rocket, to serve

Preheat your oven to 240°C/230°C fan/475°F/gas mark 9. Place a thick, flat baking tray in the oven and leave it to heat for at least 20 minutes.

Heat the oil in a frying pan over a high heat. When the oil is hot add the sliced mushrooms to the pan, and fry for 2–3 minutes, by which time the mushrooms will have wilted slightly and turned golden brown in a few places. Season with salt and pepper and remove to a plate.

Place the frying pan back over a high heat, and when hot add the spinach. Fry for about 1 minute, or until the spinach has all wilted. Season lightly with salt and pepper, then tip into a sieve. Squeeze the excess liquid from the spinach by pushing it with a wooden spoon. Keep the spinach to one side.

Generously dust a clean surface with flour. Tip your risen dough out on to the floured surface and knock the air out by kneading it for a couple of minutes. Divide the dough into four.

Take one portion of the dough and roll it out to a diameter of about 30cm, roughly the thickness of a pound coin. Do not be too concerned about making a perfect circle; I very rarely do, and as long as the dough is roughly the same thickness all over it won't make a difference to the taste or texture.

CONTINUED OVERLEAF

When you are happy with the shape dust a tray or chopping board with the polenta. Carefully lay the rolled dough out on the polenta, gently pushing the dough back into shape with your fingers.

Spread a quarter of the spinach over the base of the pizza, then add a quarter of the cooked mushrooms, finishing with a quarter of the cheese. Give the pizza a final drizzle of olive oil and season with salt and pepper.

The next bit needs to be done as quickly as you are able. Ensure that the pizza is free to move around on the polenta-dusted surface. When you're happy the pizza will slide, quickly remove the preheated tray from the oven and slip the prepared pizza straight on to it. Place the tray back in the oven and bake for 12 minutes by which time the cheese will have melted and the dough base turned crisp and lightly golden.

At this point you can start preparing your next pizza by rolling out a second ball of dough on a polenta dusted surface, and topping with tomato sauce and mozzarella.

Remove the pizza from the oven and slide straight on to a chopping board. Slip your next pizza in to the oven to keep the pizza conveyor belt running. You can either give your pizza one last drizzle of olive oil and serve immediately, or wait until the rest of the pizzas are made and serve all at once.

STUFFED CRUST PIZZA

The stuffed crust pizza is a very modern phenomenon. I was a sceptic at first but then a friend urged me to have a go at making a homemade version. I was instantly converted and now pull out the stuffed crust as a bit of a party piece.

**PREP TIME: 30 MINS,
PLUS PROVING TIME
COOKING TIME: 40 MINS**

**flour, for dusting
1 batch of Basic Dough
(see page 139)
about 2 tablespoons polenta,
for dusting
200g mozzarella for pizzas
(the stuff that comes
in a block)
200g shop-bought passata
or use 1 batch of Tomato
Sauce (see page 141)
20 slices salami
20 black olives
basil leaves, to serve**

Preheat your oven to 240°C/230°C fan/475°F/gas mark 9. Place a thick, flat baking tray in the oven and leave it to heat for at least 20 minutes.

Generously dust a clean surface with flour. Tip your risen dough out on to the floured surface and knock the air out by kneading it for a couple of minutes. Divide the dough into four.

Take one portion of the dough and roll it out to a diameter of about 30cm, roughly the thickness of a pound coin. Do not be too concerned about making a perfect circle; I very rarely do, and as long as the dough is roughly the same thickness all over it won't make a difference to the taste or texture.

When you are happy with the shape dust a tray or chopping board with the polenta. Carefully lay the rolled dough out on the polenta, gently pushing the dough back into shape with your fingers.

Take the block of mozzarella, and cut a 1cm-thick slice from it. Lay that slice down and cut it into 1cm thick lengths. Repeat this process until you have a stack of cheese sticks. Line the cheese sticks along the border of the raw dough, close to the edge, then roll the dough over the cheese and tuck it underneath all the way round to form a cheese-filled border.

Spread a couple of tablespoons of the passata over the middle of the dough, top with a few slices of salami, add some black olives, and then finally finish with a few broken up pieces of mozzarella and a few basil leaves.

The next bit needs to be done as quickly as you are able. Ensure that the pizza is free to move around on the polenta-dusted surface. When you're happy the pizza will slide, quickly remove the tray from the oven and slip the prepared pizza straight on to it. Place the tray back in the oven and bake for 12 minutes until the dough has puffed up around the edges and the cheese is bubbling and melted on the surface. While it's in the oven, prepare your next pizza.

Remove the pizza from the oven and slide straight on to a chopping board. Slip your next pizza in to the oven to keep the pizza conveyor belt running. You can either slice up your pizza and enjoy your novelty stuffed crust immediately, or alternatively wait until all the remaining pizzas are baked before handing them out to your lucky dinner guests.

CHAPTER SIX

THE
AMERICAS

North and South America are the forefather and new kid on the block of takeaway food. The North American burger is a fast-food icon with outlets spanning the globe, but the cuisines of South America are hot on its heels, with taco takeaways and samba-style restaurants popping up everywhere.

Central and South America have fresh and vibrant cuisines filled with brilliant flavour combinations: punchy coriander, mint, lime and chillies ride perfectly balanced on top of deeper, smokier, spices such as paprika and cumin. It is very easy to see why everyone is falling in love with food from this part of the world.

In contrast, North American takeaway classics like burgers and fried chicken often rely on the combination of salt and sugar to elevate the blandness of the poor ingredients so often used. It is time to look at making some of these favourites at home where we can control the freshness and quality of the produce we eat. Use the recipes in this chapter to cut through the scepticism and fall back in love with some truly great dishes.

ONION RINGS

SERVES 4

Onion rings are one of those forgotten side dishes. When reacquainted with them you remember they are absolutely delicious and swear to order them more often, only to leave it another couple of years before reminding yourself again. Let that be a thing of the past thanks to this recipe.

PREP TIME: 10 MINS
COOKING TIME: 5 MINS,
PLUS 15 MINS' SOAKING TIME

2 large onions, peeled
300ml milk
about 1 litre vegetable
or sunflower oil,
for deep-frying
50g cornflour
50g self-raising flour
1 tbsp caster sugar
100ml sparkling water
salt and freshly ground
black pepper

Take each onion in turn, and slice it crossways into 1cm-thick slices. You should be able to make about 5 slices.

Pick up each slice, and separate the layers to create separate rings of onion. Repeat the process with the second onion. Place the rings of onion in a bowl and pour over the milk. Leave the onions to soak for a minimum of 15 minutes.

Drain the onions through a colander, discarding the milk. Tip the onions on to a large tray or plate. Heat the oil in a large, deep saucepan pan or a deep fryer to 180°C.

Mix together the cornflour and self-raising flour and season generously with salt and pepper. Sprinkle a tablespoon of the mixed flour over the soaked onion rings, and then use your hands to mix the onions around.

Add the caster sugar to the remaining flour mixture. Pour in the sparkling water, whisking as you add it. Continue whisking until you form a smooth batter.

Taking a small handful of floured onion rings, drop them into the batter and then one by one, carefully lower them into the hot oil. Fry the onion rings for 1 minute, by which time the batter should be crisp and golden.

Remove the cooked rings with a slotted spoon to a piece of kitchen paper to drain any excess oil. Keep the cooked onion rings warm in a low oven whilst you cook the remainder. Season with a little salt before serving.

FRIED CHICKEN

★
—————

Frying chicken has become something of an obsession of mine. I, probably like many of you, find fried chicken irresistible, so to tempt both myself and you from the chicken shops I have devoted many hours in pursuit of the perfect homemade, healthier version of the takeaway. This chicken is brilliant because it isn't filled with salts and sugars yet it doesn't compromise on flavour.

PREP TIME: 25 MINS
COOKING TIME: 15 MINS
PLUS MARINATING TIME

400ml milk
1 large onion,
    roughly chopped
2 tbsp black peppercorns
3 sticks celery,
    roughly chopped
6 cloves garlic,
    roughly bashed
6 skinless chicken legs,
    with bone
6 skinless chicken thighs,
    with bone
400g plain flour
1 tbsp smoked paprika
vegetable or sunflower oil,
    for frying
salt and freshly ground
    black pepper
American Slaw (see page
    159), to serve (optional)
Shoestring Fries (see page
    167), to serve (optional)

Pour the milk along with 400ml water into a saucepan, and add the onion, peppercorns, celery and garlic. Place the pan over a high heat and bring to the boil. As soon as the milk has boiled remove from the heat and leave to cool to room temperature.

Place the chicken legs and tights in a large dish and when the milk has cooled pour it over the chicken, ensuring that as much of the chicken is immersed as possible. Cover the chicken and leave it in the fridge to marinate overnight. Remove the chicken from the fridge an hour before you plan on cooking it to let it come back to room temperature.

When ready to cook, drain the chicken, discarding the milk and the vegetables.

Tip the flour on to a large plate or tray, add the smoked paprika, along with a generous amount of salt and pepper and mix to combine.

Pour about 4cm of oil into a high-sided frying pan for which you have a lid and place over a medium-high heat. You are aiming to reach a temperature of 170°C (a cube of bread should take 40 seconds to brown at this temperature).

Taking each piece of chicken in turn, shake it roughly dry before dropping it into the seasoned flour. With light fingers roll the chicken piece around in the flour, before picking up

CONTINUED OVERLEAF

and shaking off excess flour with a gentle tap of your hands. Place the floured chicken to one side whilst you repeat the process with the remainder.

When all of the chicken pieces are coated and the oil is hot, carefully lower each piece of chicken into the oil. The oil should come halfway up the chicken pieces and bubble almost instantly. Depending on the size of your pan you will most likely have to cook the chicken in two batches. Do not overload the pan; try to give each piece of chicken a margin of about about 3cm of space.

Fry each batch of chicken pieces with the lid on for 5 minutes. Take the lid off, and use a pair of long tongs to turn the pieces over. Replace the lid and fry for a further 5 minutes.

The chicken should how have turned a deep brown and be cooked all the way through to the bone. Check this by cutting open one of the larger pieces of chicken and ensuring the flesh has changed from pink to white. When you are satisfied the pieces are thoroughly cooked, remove them on to a piece of clean kitchen paper to drain off any excess oil. If you are cooking in batches, place the cooked chicken into a warm oven whilst you finish cooking the rest.

Serve up your fried chicken, with the coleslaw and fries if you like.

AMERICAN SLAW

This slaw is unashamedly based on the classic American Waldorf salad. It is the slaw to go with anything and everything. Use almost any type of apple in this recipe, from the super-sweet Braeburn to the more complex, tart varieties like Granny Smith. Each brings a different, but still delicious characteristic to the slaw.

PREP TIME: 15 MINS
COOKING TIME: 0 MINS

6 heaped tablespoons
   mayonnaise
2 tbsp white wine vinegar
½ large white cabbage,
   cored and shredded
½ red onion, very
   finely sliced
2 apples, peeled,
   cored and grated
1 carrot, grated
40g walnuts, roughly
   broken up
40g raisins
salt and freshly ground
   black pepper

Dollop the mayonnaise into a large bowl and add the vinegar. Mix until fully combined.

Add the rest of the ingredients to the bowl, along with a pinch of salt and a generous grind of pepper. Mix together thoroughly and serve.

BARBECUE RIBS

★

SERVES 4

Tender pork meat prised from the bone is wonderfully satisfying and when that meat is smothered with barbecue sauce and lightly charred it is even better. I like to tenderise my meat by boiling it before passing it over the barbecue or through the oven, but it isn't totally necessary. The barbecue sauce in this recipe should not be limited to pork ribs; it works very well as a marinade for other meats or served alongside or on top of almost any grilled or barbecued meat.

PREP TIME: 15 MINS
COOKING TIME: 1 HOUR 30 MINS

6 racks of baby back ribs
  (about 2kg)
400ml pineapple juice
2 onions, roughly chopped
2 sprigs oregano or
  2 tbsp dried oregano
6 tbsp tomato ketchup
2 tbsp light soft brown sugar
1 tsp smoked paprika
6 tbsp Worcestershire sauce
2 tbsp clear honey
American slaw (see page
  159), to serve

Place the pork ribs in a large saucepan. Pour over the pineapple juice, then top up the liquid with water until the ribs are covered. Add the onions and oregano to the pan.

Bring the liquid to the boil, skimming off any scum that floats to the surface. Reduce the heat to a simmer and cook the ribs like this for 1 hour. After an hour turn the heat off and let the meat rest in the warm liquid for 10 minutes.

Preheat your oven to 200°C/190°C fan/400°F/gas mark 6.

Mix together the tomato ketchup, brown sugar, paprika, Worcestershire sauce and honey until they have been completely combined into one delicious barbecue sauce.

Line a roasting tray with foil, then lay the cooked ribs on the tray, shaking off as much excess liquid as possible. Pour the barbecue sauce over the ribs swishing them around in the sauce to ensure they are well covered.

Place the tray in the oven and roast for 20 minutes, turning and basting a couple of time whilst cooking. Remove the ribs from the oven, and either split into individual ribs or serve as whole racks with the slaw on the side.

MACARONI CHEESE

★
_____

SERVES 4

There are many additions that can be made to this recipe, from the inclusion of bacon and tomato slices to truffle oil. However, I like to keep things simple and have opted for beautiful, oompa-loompa coloured simplicity. If you can't find the onion or garlic salt, you can bring the milk for the white sauce to the boil with a couple of peeled garlic cloves and a peeled, halved onion in it. Discard them before adding the milk to the flour mixture.

PREP TIME: 20 MINS
COOKING TIME: 35 MINS

600g dried macaroni
2 tbsp olive oil
80g unsalted butter
80g plain flour
800ml milk
150g red Leicester, grated
1 tsp mustard powder
1 tsp onion salt
1 tsp garlic salt
20g Parmesan, grated
salt and freshly ground
**   black pepper**
green salad, to serve (if
**   you're feeling virtuous)**

Cook the pasta according to the packet instructions. Drain in a colander, then run it under cold water to cool it completely. Tip the pasta into a large bowl and pour in the oil along with a pinch of salt and pepper. Mix well.

Preheat your oven to 200°C/190°C fan/400°F/gas mark 6.

Place the butter in a large saucepan over a medium-high heat. When the butter has melted, reduce the heat and tip in the flour. As soon as the flour is in the pan, begin to stir with a wooden spoon. Cook the mixture for 1 minute, stirring almost constantly – you are aiming for a smooth paste.

Take the saucepan off the heat and pour in roughly a quarter of the milk. Mix until completely combined. Don't worry if the ingredients begin to clump a bit. Add half the remaining liquid and place the pan back on the hob, stirring almost continuously. When the milk has been worked in, pour in the remainder and continue to stir. You need to bring the sauce to the boil, whilst stirring. Let the sauce boil for 1 minute, before reducing the heat to medium and adding the cheese. Stir well, until all of the cheese has been combined into the sauce.

Remove the sauce from the heat and add the mustard powder and onion and garlic salts. Stir to combine.

Tip the pasta into the sauce and stir well to coat with the mixture. Tip into an ovenproof dish. Scatter the Parmesan over the top and bake for 15–20 minutes, by which time the sauce will have turned golden in places and will be bubbling gloriously around the edges.

ULTIMATE BURGER

★

SERVES 2

You will find no onion, egg or breadcrumbs in these burgers, just unadulterated seasoned minced meat. I suggest serving these burgers with my burger sauce, sliced tomatoes, sliced gherkins and lettuce, but that's just how I like mine. Feel free to engineer your own signature burgers, topping them with anything from kimchi to macaroni cheese. This recipe takes advantage of the way meat comes out of the mincing machine. By lining up the strands of the minced beef, and then ensuring the burgers are cut against the grain before frying, the meat gives very little natural resistance when bitten into – rendering it satisfyingly tender.

PREP TIME: 15 MINS
COOKING TIME: 8 MINS
FOR MEDIUM-RARE

1kg best-quality minced beef, purchased as two 500g packets
a little sunflower or vegetable oil, for frying
4 burger buns
slices of your favourite cheese (optional)
salt and freshly ground black pepper
sliced gherkins, to serve
lettuce leaves, to serve
sliced tomatoes, to serve
Shoestring Fries (see page 167), to serve

For the burger sauce
3 heaped tablespoons mayonnaise
2 heaped tablespoons tomato relish (any shop-bought variety will do)
1 small banana shallot, finely diced
pinch of caster sugar
2 tsp white wine vinegar

With a chopping board in front of you, place your cling film box at the far edge of the board. Draw the cling film over the chopping board towards you, resting the edge of the cling film on the edge of the board closest to you. Don't cut the cling film.

Unwrap the packets of mince. Pick up one block of mince and lay it in the middle of your cling-lined chopping board. Place the second block of minced beef on top of the first.

Lift up the edge of cling film closest to you and fold it over the meat, then roll the meat up in cling film, using a little pressure to bring the mince together, but not too much that it starts escaping from the open ends. Roll the mince until it is well encased in more layers of cling film.

Grab both ends of the cling film and holding them tightly, roll the whole block of mince into a large sausage shape, then tie a knot at each end of the cling. Place your 'beef sausage' in the fridge, and leave for a minimum of 4 hours but preferably overnight.

When ready to cook, remove the sausage from the fridge. Slice the ends off, cutting straight through the cling film, then slice the remainder into four large burger patties, again cutting through the film. Carefully remove the cling

CONTINUED OVERLEAF

shroud from each burger and lightly push the meat out to a thickness of about 2.5cm.

Preheat your oven to its lowest setting.

Heat a griddle pan over a high heat. If you don't have a griddle pan, use a large frying pan or better still a barbecue. Rub a little oil on to the burgers and season generously with salt and pepper.

When the griddle is hot, add the burgers and fry for 3 minutes. Flip the burgers and fry for a further 3 minutes. Slide your burgers on to an oven tray, and leave to rest in the warm oven for 5 minutes. If you want a cheeseburger this is the time to adorn the burgers with a slice of your favourite cheese. Whilst the burgers are resting, griddle your buns.

For the burger sauce, simply mix all of the ingredients until they are fully combined. Set aside until ready to serve.

Construct your burger: for me that's with lashings of burger sauce, gherkins, lettuce and tomatoes; a portion of shoestring fries alongside.

SHOESTRING FRIES

★

SERVES 4

These are those thin fries that are served in huge crispy mounds alongside everything from burgers to mussels. Because of their thinness and the double frying method they are incredibly crisp, making them the perfect accompaniment to the soft bun and tender burger. The most important but annoyingly arduous part of this recipe is cutting the potatoes to the requisite size. I'm afraid it comes down to spending a bit of time with a sharp knife; I suggest flipping on the Beach Boys and letting your mind wander.

PREP TIME: 20 MINS
COOKING TIME: 5 MINS,
PLUS DRYING TIME

**4 large floury potatoes,
such as Maris Piper,
peeled
about 1 litre vegetable
or sunflower oil,
for deep-frying
salt**

Take each potato in turn, and using a knife or a mandolin slice the potato into long matchsticks about 5mm thick. This may take a little time but consider it therapeutic.

When you have chipped all of the potatoes place the pieces in a large bowl of cold water. Swoosh the potatoes around, then drain. Refill the bowl with water, swoosh, and drain again. Repeat this process another two times. This is to remove starch from the potatoes.

Drain the potatoes through a colander and shake to extract as much excess liquid as possible. When you have removed as much liquid as you can, tip the potatoes on to a tray lined with a clean tea towel. Spread them evenly over the lined tray then place it in the fridge. Leave the chips to cool and dry for 1 hour.

When ready to cook, pour the oil into a large saucepan or a deep fryer and heat to 170°C (a cube of bread should take about 40 seconds to brown at this temperature). Add the potatoes and fry for 1 minute, before carefully spooning out the blanched chips with a slotted spoon and draining on greaseproof paper. It is likely that you will have to blanch your chips in two batches.

Just before serving, heat the oil to 190°C (a cube of bread should brown in about 20 seconds). Fry your blanched potatoes, again in batches if needed, for 1 minute. They should crisp and turn golden. Tip the chips straight on to kitchen paper to drain excess oil and salt generously.

CHICKEN WINGS
(BUFFALOS DON'T HAVE WINGS)

★
———

SERVES 4

Chicken wings are so very cheap yet so very tasty. They are the perfect snack to be enjoyed at almost any occasion. My version is also a little healthier as the wings are roasted instead of deep-fried. Leaving you with no excuse not to cook them at home.

PREP TIME: 15 MINS
COOKING TIME: 25 MINS

**5 tbsp sunflower
   or vegetable oil**
150g plain flour
1 tbsp cayenne pepper
1 tbsp celery salt
1 tbsp garlic salt
1 tbsp onion salt
16 chicken wings
**Blue Cheese Dressing,
   (see page 171) to serve**
celery sticks, to serve

Preheat your oven to 200°C/190°C fan/400°F/gas mark 6.

Pour the oil into a large roasting tray, then place in the oven to heat whilst you prepare the rest of the recipe.

Place the flour, cayenne pepper, and all the flavoured salts into a large freezer bag and shake to mix thoroughly.

Drop the chicken wing pieces into the bag and scrunch them around to ensure all of the chicken pieces are well coated in the flour mixture.

Tip the coated wings from the bag into a dry colander, and give them a good shake over the sink to ensure that excess flour is removed.

Remove preheated tray from the oven and carefully tip the floured chicken into the hot oil. The wings should sizzle and bubble a little as they hit the oil. Place the tray back in the oven and roast for 10 minutes. Remove the tray and turn the chicken, then roast for a further 15 minutes.

Remove the chicken wings from the oven, stack them on a plate and serve with the blue cheese sauce and celery sticks. Take a seat on your sofa and search out some American Football.

THREE AMERICAN DRESSINGS

I've taken my three favourite classic American dressings and have tried to give you a quick and easy version of each for a simple yet authentic American experience. All can be kept for up to 4 days in an airtight container in the fridge.

CAESAR

SERVES 4

The Caesar salad is not named after the famous Emperor, but instead, a rather more humble Italian immigrant to America named Caesar Cardini. He first served his creation in his restaurant in the 1920s. There are many elaborate stories as to why and how he threw together the ingredients to create the first Caesar salad, but my guess is that he was just quite a good chef who made a damn fine dressing. My shortcut version does away with the most arduous part of the process by using shop-bought mayonnaise.

PREP TIME: 5 MINS
COOKING TIME: 0 MINS

8 tbsp good-quality shop-bought mayonnaise
5 anchovies from a jar, drained
3 tbsp grated Parmesan
1 clove garlic, minced
2 tbsp warm water

Place all of the ingredients in a small food processor, and blitz until smooth. If you don't have a small food processor, use a pestle and mortar, and if you don't have a pestle and mortar, just ensure you chop all of the ingredients as finely as you can, and use a whisk to vigorously mix.

BLUE CHEESE

SERVES 4

Blue cheese may be European but the Americans have truly embraced it as a dressing for anything, from a robust, chunky salad to chicken wings.

PREPARATION TIME: 2 MINUTES
COOKING TIME: 0 MINUTES

150g Gorgonzola cheese
100ml buttermilk
4 tbsp Worcestershire sauce
1 tsp sugar

Place all of the ingredients in a small food processor and blitz until smooth (or see recipe opposite for alternative methods).

RANCH

SERVES 4

Ranch dressing is so called because it was invented by a couple who owned a commercial ranch that would put on horse-riding experiences for city slickers searching for a little weekend adventure. Legend has it that very soon people were visiting not only to experience beautiful, uninterrupted sunsets and the smell of horse dung in the mornings but for another taste of the moreish dressing.

PREPARATION TIME: 5 MINUTES
COOKING TIME: 0 MINUTES

200g good-quality shop-
    bought mayonnaise
100g buttermilk
1 clove garlic, minced
2 tbsp finely chopped chives
2 tbsp finely chopped parsley
2 tsp roughly chopped
    thyme leaves
1 tsp garlic salt
1 tsp onion salt

Place all of the ingredients in a small food processor and blitz until smooth (or see recipe opposite for alternative methods).

CHILLI MEXICAN EGGS

SERVES 4

Sometimes you wake up, the sun is shining, and you feel a rejuvenated vigour for life and that vigour needs feeding. Cereal is part of your weekday routine and toast is far too mundane; what you want and what you need is some chilli – some spice to spark the taste buds, which in turn will stimulate your mind. This recipe is the perfect fuel to put a huge smile on your face and set you up for the day ahead.

PREP TIME: 10 MINS
COOKING TIME: 5–6 MINS

8 eggs
3 tbsp vegetable oil
1 green pepper, deseeded and cut into 1cm slices
1 red onion, peeled and roughly diced
2 red chillies, roughly diced (leave the seeds in for an extra kick)
a few leaves of coriander, to serve
freshly ground black pepper
ketchup, to serve (optional)
chilli sauce, to serve (optional)

Crack the eggs into a large bowl and whisk well with a fork until the whites and yolks are fully combined.

Heat the oil in a large, non-stick frying pan over a high heat. When hot add the green pepper and red onion. Fry, stirring occasionally, for about 2 minutes, by which time some of the pieces should be lightly scorched.

Add the red chillies and continue to stir and fry for a further 30 seconds, before pouring in the beaten eggs.

Leave the eggs to settle, then let them fry for about 30 seconds without any stirring at all. After about 30 seconds the egg should begin to set around the edges. Draw the egg in from the outside into the middle, and as you do, flip some of the egg over, and continue to fry, moving it only occasionally for another 2 minutes. You are aiming for some of the egg to be browned, but also for some of it to still be a little 'loose', this is done by not over stirring.

Divide the eggs between two plates, top with a few leaves of coriander, a generous grind of black pepper, and serve with a mixture of ketchup and chilli sauce, if liked.

Devour your eggs, feel a stirring of mischief and consider a shot of tequila to really set you up for the day.

STEAK and SALSA BURRITO

★

SERVES 4

This is one of my favourite recipes in the book. The combination of flavours and textures is almost perfect. Having eaten this I'm not sure why anyone bothers spending a fortune on Michelin-star restaurants when food at home can taste this good. I have opted to cook the meat in two large steaks as I think the result is better, especially if you prefer your meat medium to rare. But if you are in a rush, simply slice the steaks into strips and stir-fry them.

PREP TIME: 15 MINS,
PLUS MARINATING TIME
COOKING TIME: 12 MINS

100ml orange juice
1 tbsp dried oregano
2 cloves garlic, minced
2 tbsp light soy sauce
1 tbsp light brown sugar
2 x 250g sirloin steaks
4–6 flour tortilla wraps (the
    quantity depends on how
    well you can pack yours)
½ iceberg lettuce, shredded
salt and freshly ground
    black pepper
soured cream, to serve
grated Cheddar cheese,
    to serve
The Best Guacamole
    (see page 177), to serve

For the salsa
2 large, ripe tomatoes
½ red onion, finely diced
4 tbsp chopped coriander
juice of 2 limes
2 tbsp red wine vinegar

Pour the orange juice into a large dish and add the oregano, garlic, soy sauce and sugar. Use a spoon to mix the ingredients thoroughly until fully combined. Lay the steaks in the marinade and spoon some of the mixture over the top. Cover the steaks and place in the fridge to marinate for a minimum of 1 hour but preferably overnight, ensuring you turn them in the marinade every now and again.

About an hour before you want to serve your burritos, remove the steaks from the fridge, and let them come up to room temperature. It is now time to make your salsa. Roughly chop the tomatoes into 2cm pieces. Scoop the flesh, along with all the juice and seeds from the board into a bowl and add the red onion, coriander, lime juice, red wine vinegar and a generous amount of salt and black pepper. Stir the ingredients until they are well mixed. Leave to one side.

Preheat your grill to maximum.

Remove the steaks from the marinade, sliding your fingers down the meat to try and remove excess marinade. Lay the steaks on your grill tray, and place the steaks close to the elements. Leave the steaks to cook for 3 minutes, before flipping over and grilling for a further 3 minutes. Remove

CONTINUED OVERLEAF

the steaks from the grill, and swish back through the marinade, before grilling for a further 2 minutes on each side. Remove the steaks to a plate, and leave to rest for at least 5 minutes.

Warm up your tortilla wraps, either wrapped in foil in the oven or in a dry frying pan.

After the steaks have had their resting time, slice into thick pieces, and construct your burrito. Serve with the guacamole alongside. You can attempt to eat your burrito neatly with a knife and fork but I suggest grabbing hold with both hands and stuffing it directly into your mouth.

THE BEST GUACAMOLE

SERVES 4

It is not often I boast, but this is such a good recipe that I feel confident in giving it the presumptive title of 'The Best'. For this recipe, I have not confined myself within the borders of America when considering ingredients and have therefore included a couple of dashes of Asia to complement the delicious nuttiness of avocado. Have a go, you won't look back.

PREP TIME: 10 MINS
COOKING TIME: 0 MINS

3 large, ripe Hass avocados,
  peeled and roughly
  chopped into 2cm pieces
1 red chilli, deseeded
  and finely diced
1 small red onion,
  finely diced
3 tbsp coriander leaves,
  roughly chopped
juice of 2 limes
3 tsp fish sauce
1 tsp sesame oil
salt and freshly ground
  black pepper

Place all of the ingredients into a large mixing bowl along with a generous pinch of salt and pepper.

Use a fork to mix the ingredients – it should cut into the avocado flesh as you mix. You are aiming for a rough mixture, with no singular large pieces but some texture. You don't need to obsess about the texture; as long as all of the ingredients are thoroughly mixed the guacamole will taste delicious.

Serve the guacamole with almost anything, from tortilla chips to roast chicken.

EASY TORTILLA CHIPS

SERVES 4

Tortilla chips from the packet are undeniably delicious, in fact they are more than that, they are positively addictive. As much as we all enjoy eating a couple of crisps, which soon become a small handful and then eventually the whole packet, we know they are not good for us, and that their moreish quality isn't totally natural. By making your own chips you can not only reduce the amount of salt and oil used, but once you have become familiar with the cooking process you can tailor the flavour combination to suit your tastes. My tortilla chips take minutes to cook and are perfect loaded with guacamole or salsa.

PREP TIME: 3 MINS
COOKING TIME: 8 MINS

4 corn tortilla wraps
olive oil, for drizzling
pinch of ground coriander
pinch of paprika
pinch of ground cumin
salt and freshly ground
**   black pepper**
dips of your choice, to serve

Preheat your oven to 190°C/fan 180°C/375°F/gas mark 5.

Take the tortilla wraps one at a time, and with a sharp knife or scissors, cut triangles roughly the size and shape of packet tortilla chips – don't worry about being exact. Repeat the process with the remaining wraps.

Spread the cut shapes out on a baking sheet, ensuring they are not overlapping; if necessary, use a second sheet. Drizzle the tortillas with the olive oil so that every piece has a little oil on it.

Mix together the coriander, paprika and cumin along with a generous amount of both salt and pepper, and then sprinkle the spice mixture as evenly as possible over the tortillas. Place your tray(s) in the oven and bake for 6–8 minutes, by which time the tortillas will be crisp and golden brown.

Remove the tortilla chips from the oven and serve with dips. Enjoy being able to control your tortilla intake.

FRIJOLES and CHEESE

★
___

SERVES 4

If you've ever been lucky enough to go to Mexico then I'm pretty sure you would have come across this delicious dish made with black beans. I'm guessing that you would have presumed that the ingredients would be too tricky to source back at home. Well surprise, surprise black beans are available in most supermarkets and the crumbly cheese on top can be easily replicated using a local alternative. So grab yourself a cold Corona, cook up this recipe and feel the warmth of Mexico flooding into your home... Into your mouth at least.

PREP TIME: 10 MINS
COOKING TIME: 10 MINS

large knob of butter
1 onion, diced
2 cloves garlic,
finely chopped
1 red chilli, deseeded
and finely diced
1 x 400g tin black beans,
drained and rinsed
5 tbsp vegetable stock
½ bunch of coriander –
half chopped; the other
half left as whole leaves
500g Lancashire cheese
Easy Tortilla Chips
(see page 178), to serve
The Best Guacamole
(see page 177), to serve

Melt the butter in a medium saucepan over a medium-high heat and add the onion. Fry for 5 minutes, stirring regularly; the onion should soften without colouring.

Add the garlic and chilli and continue to fry over medium heat for 2 minutes. Add the black beans and stir to mix. Pour in the vegetable stock and the chopped coriander. Bring the stock to the boil, before reducing the heat to a simmer and cooking like this for about 3 minutes or until the beans become tender.

Take the pan off the heat and use a potato masher to crush the beans – you are not looking to make a purée, but do try to bash up all the beans.

Pour the beans into a serving dish, crumble over the cheese and garnish with the whole coriander leaves. Serve with the tortilla chips and guacamole.

SEA BASS TARTARE TOSTADA

SERVES 4

This dish is perfect for summer evenings when you want something just a little different that is not only quick and easy but also packs a serious punch. If you find it tricky to source sea bass then both tuna and salmon work just as well as alternatives, just make sure whatever fish you choose is as fresh as possible.

PREP TIME: 15 MINS
COOKING TIME: 6–8 MINS

4 tbsp red wine vinegar
7 coriander seeds, lightly crushed in a pestle and mortar or under the blade of your knife
3 tbsp light olive oil, plus some extra for drizzling
1 red chilli, deseeded and finely diced
½ bunch of chives, finely sliced
¼ bunch of parsley, finely chopped
Easy Tortilla Chips (see page 178)
400g very fresh skinless sea bass fillets
3 tbsp shelled pistachio nuts, toasted and roughly chopped

Preheat your oven to 200°C/190°C fan/400°F/gas mark 6.

Pour the red wine vinegar into a bowl and add the coriander seeds, olive oil, red chilli, chives and parsley. Roughly mix the ingredients together and leave to stand whilst you continue with the rest of the recipe.

Make your tortilla chips at this point, following the recipe on page 178.

Use your sharpest knife to cut the sea bass into 1cm cubes – don't worry about being exact here, the most important thing is that the pieces are quite small.

Place the fish into a bowl and pour over the vinegar mixture. Gently mix the liquid and herbs in with the fish, being careful not to be so vigorous as to break up the pieces of fish.

Spoon the tartare into a bowl, top with a few pistachio pieces and serve with the tortilla chips.

CHORIZO, SPINACH and POTATO QUESADILLA

★

SERVES 2

Quesadillas are like the South American version of a cheese toastie, and like the toastie they are the perfect comfort food for every desperate situation, from a broken heart to a hangover. I have chosen a delicious chorizo and potato filling that is unbelievably satisfying, however almost any combination of ingredients you would put in a toastie can also be stuffed into a quesadilla – from ham and cheese to chocolate spread and banana.

PREP TIME: 15 MINS
COOKING TIME: 15 MINS

1 tbsp oil
200g cooking chorizo,
    cut into 1cm cubes
225g new potatoes, boiled
    until tender and roughly
    chopped into small pieces
4 spring onions, trimmed
    and sliced 1cm thick
2 large handfuls baby
    leaf spinach
juice of ½ lemon
2 large flour tortilla wraps
75g cheese, such as grated
    Cheddar, torn mozzarella
    or crumbled Lancashire
    cheese
salt and freshly ground
    black pepper
rocket, to serve (optional)

Heat the oil in a large frying pan over a medium-high heat. When hot tip in the chorizo and fry, stirring regularly, for 2–3 minutes, by which time the chorizo should have rendered some of its delicious red oil. If it hasn't, continue to fry.

Remove the pan from the heat and leaving as much of the ruby oil in the pan as possible spoon the cooked chorizo on to a plate and keep to one side.

Replace the pan on the hob and increase the heat to maximum. When the oil is nice and hot tip in the potato pieces. Fry the potatoes for 4–5 minutes, until they pick up a little colour. It is important not to stir the potatoes too often whilst frying, otherwise they will take an age to colour.

When you are happy with the potatoes, reduce the heat to medium and add the spring onions, tossing together with the potatoes. Fry for 30 seconds before tipping the cooked chorizo back into the pan.

Drop the spinach leaves into the pan and gradually fold in with the rest of the ingredients. Turn the heat off but continue to stir the ingredients, using the residual heat in the pan to finish wilting the spinach. Season the mixture with the lemon juice and a little salt and pepper. Give the mix one final stir before tipping it into a large bowl.

Wipe the pan clean, then put it back on a medium-high heat. Place one of the tortillas in the base of the frying pan. Spoon the cooked chorizo mixture on to the warming wrap, squeezing off as much excess liquid off as you can. Top the mixture with your choice of cheese, and then place the second tortilla wrap on top of the mixture, pushing it down gently with the palm of your hand. Leave the quesadilla to cook like this for 1 minute.

To flip the quesadilla, place a large plate on top, and then with one hand on the plate, and the other on the frying pan handle, flip the quesadilla on to the plate. Place the frying pan back on the heat and then slide the quesadilla back into the pan on its uncooked side. Continue to cook for a further 2–3 minutes on that side.

When cooked slide the quesadilla on to a board, slice into segments, top with rocket, if liked, and with every mouthful feel the stress of life slowly melt away.

CHAPTER
SEVEN ➤

* BRITISH *

As a nation known for beer, football and fish 'n' chips you may wonder what Great Britain has to offer the rest of the world in the way of culinary expertise. I assure you there is far more to the British chippie than battered fish and thick chips. Pies, kebabs, fish cakes and sausage rolls are all there waiting for you in the hot cupboard.

When properly executed, fish 'n' chips rightly earns its place in the takeaway food hall of fame: perfectly steamed fish encased in a crisply fried golden jacket, accompanied by thick-cut robust chips, all drenched in salt and vinegar and accompanied by deeply savoury mushy peas. It is quite simply a winning combination. There is virtually nothing that could be changed to improve this classic takeaway meal... Apart from using the best ingredients and cooking in fresh oil.

Many chip shops change their oil too infrequently which results in the ingredients frying at a lower temperature than intended. This means the fish and potatoes don't crisp immediately so they absorb oil and the whole meal is therefore heavy and hard to digest.

Try the following version of fish 'n' chips to see what it can be, then flick on and you will see how much more British takeaway cuisine has to offer.

CLASSIC FISH 'N' CHIPS
and TARTARE SAUCE

Fish 'n' chips is the classic takeaway that holds a very special place in the hearts of those brought up in Britain. A trip to the chippie is a great British tradition, and long may it stand. However over time the quality of food served up has declined, with proprietors opting for frozen fish and pre-made batters; it seems they are more interested in profit margins than quality produce. It is now harder than ever to find a decent chip shop meaning there is no better time to try cooking your beloved fish 'n' chips at home.

PREP TIME: 25 MINS
COOKING TIME: 35 MINS

about 1.5 litres of vegetable
   or sunflower oil,
   for deep-frying
4 floury potatoes, peeled
200g self-raising flour, plus
   a little extra for dusting
2 tsp salt
250–300ml lager (I use
   Heineken)
4 x 200g pieces of thick
   cod, haddock or pollock
   fillet, skinned
malt vinegar, to serve

For the tartare sauce
6 heaped tablespoons
   good-quality mayonnaise
juice of 1 lemon
1 large shallot, finely diced
2 tbsp capers, roughly
   chopped
1 large gherkin, finely
   chopped
2 tbsp chopped parsley

Heat 20cm of oil in a large, high-sided saucepan or deep fryer to 160°C. If you don't have a thermometer then you can tell when the oil is at 160°C by dropping a cube of bread into it; the bread should be golden brown in about 1 minute.

Slice each potato into chips roughly 2cm thick. Carefully lower the chipped potatoes into the hot oil. Fry for 7 minutes at this low temperature before removing with a slotted spoon and tipping on to a tray or plate lined with baking parchment. Leave these blanched chips in a cool place until ready to fry again.

Prepare the tartare sauce. Spoon the mayonnaise into a bowl and add the lemon juice, shallot, capers, gherkin and parsley and mix until all the ingredients are well combined. Cover the sauce and place in the fridge until ready to eat.

Increase the oil temperature to 170°C – your bread should take 40 seconds to brown at this temperature.

Tip the flour into a large bowl and add 1 teaspoon of the salt. Pour the lager slowly into the flour whilst whisking. Work the lager into the flour until you reach a batter with the consistency of thick double cream.

CONTINUED OVERLEAF

Preheat your oven to its lowest setting. Line an oven tray with baking parchment.

Scatter some of the extra flour on to a plate or tray, and season generously with salt. Take each piece of fish in turn and dust in the seasoned flour. Pat the fish with your hand to remove excess flour – you're after a thin coating.

When your oil has reached the correct temperature, again, working with one piece of fish at a time, dip the floured fillets in the batter, shaking off excess batter, then gently lower into the hot oil. It is probable that you will only be able to cook two pieces at a time. Fry the fish for 9 minutes, by which time the batter should have turned crisp and golden. Transfer the fish to the lined tray and place in the warm oven. Repeat the process with the remaining fish.

Increase the heat of the oil to 180°C – your bread should take about 30 seconds to brown at this temperature.

Drop your blanched chips into the hot oil, and fry for 2 minutes until the chips have turned golden and crisp. Remove the chips with a slotted spoon and season with a generous smattering of salt.

Serve up your fish 'n' chips with a generous amount of malt vinegar, if liked, and wooden forks for that authentic chippie feel.

SAUSAGE ROLL

SERVES 4

The sausage roll is close to the perfect snack: homely soft sausage meat encased in delicately flaky, delicious puff pastry. My sausage rolls contain a few tasty surprises added to the basic sausage filling that help elevate flavour and texture above anything you would find in a takeaway.

PREP TIME: 40 MINS
COOKING TIME: 45 MINS

generous knob of butter
2 shallots, finely diced
2 sprigs of thyme
5 sage leaves, finely chopped
12 good-quality sausages
6 tbsp fresh breadcrumbs
40g dried cranberries,
roughly chopped
40g pistachio nuts, shelled
and roughly chopped
2 eggs
plain flour, for dusting
1 x 500g block puff pastry
salt and freshly ground
black pepper

Preheat your oven to 180°C/fan 170°C/350°F/gas mark 4. Line a baking tray with baking parchment.

Melt the butter in small frying pan over a medium-high heat until bubbling lightly, then add the shallots and thyme sprigs. Fry for about 3 minutes, stirring regularly. The shallots will turn opaque and soft; when this happens, remove the pan from the heat and add the chopped sage. Mix with the rest of the ingredients and set aside to cool.

Take a sausage and squeeze the meat from the casing into a bowl by applying a little pressure at one end. Discard the casing and repeat the process with the rest of the sausages.

Add the breadcrumbs, cranberries and pistachio nuts to the sausage meat along with one of the eggs and a little salt and pepper. Tip the cooled shallot mixture into the bowl. Mix all of the ingredients together until they are fully combined; I find the best tool for this job is my hands.

Lightly dust a clean surface with some flour. Roll your block of pastry into a rough rectangle, about 35 x 20cm and 5mm thick. Square the edges off with a knife.

Using your hands, pack the sausage mixture in a line down the centre of the pastry from the very top to the bottom. Fold one of the long sides over the meat in the middle, and lay it loosely on top of the opposite side. Use the edge of your palm to push the pastry tight against the sausage mixture to form

CONTINUED OVERLEAF

a huge sausage roll. On the side where the two edges of pastry meat there will be some excess pastry which you should slice off, leaving just enough pastry to join together. If so inclined crimp the join.

Slash the top of the sausage roll with a knife in about 5 different places before beating the remaining egg and brushing it over the roll. Carefully slide your sausage roll on to the prepared tray and place it in the oven.

Bake the sausage roll for 35–40 minutes by which time the pastry will have turned a tempting golden hue, and the meat will be cooked through. To ensure the meat is fully cooked, push a sharp knife into the thickest part of the sausage roll and leave it for 5 seconds. Touch the tip of the knife and if it's hot then the meat is fully cooked.

Enjoy your sausage roll hot or cold, for a main meal or as a snack with others, or on your own – this is a dish for any occasion. If you would prefer to make smaller sausage rolls then cut the rolled pastry into smaller rectangles, and divide the mixture evenly before closing and crimping

CHICKEN SHISH KEBAB

SERVES 4

The chicken shish kebab is a wonderful example of a dish from another very different country becoming so popular in its adopted country that its place on the menu is no longer seen as exotic, rather expected. The chicken shish originates from Turkey, yet we have taken to it in Britain so well that it has become a chip-shop staple. This recipe uses chicken thighs crammed together on to skewers, a method that preserves the natural juiciness of the meat.

PREP TIME: 20 MINS,
PLUS MARINATING TIME
COOKING TIME: 25 MINS

150g Greek yoghurt
2 tbsp tomato purée
juice of 1 lemon
3 tsp ground cumin
1 tsp smoked paprika
4 cloves garlic, minced
10 skinless, boneless
   chicken thighs
1 small bunch of parsley,
   leaves only
1 small bunch of mint,
   leaves only
2 large tomatoes,
   roughly chopped
salt and freshly ground
   black pepper
4 toasted pitta breads
   or flat breads, to serve
chilli sauce, to serve
   (optional)

Pour the yoghurt into a bowl and add the tomato purée, lemon juice, ground cumin, paprika and garlic along with a generous amount of both salt and pepper. Mix the ingredients thoroughly to make a smooth paste.

Add the chicken thighs to the yoghurt mixture, and mix well to ensure the chicken is well covered. Leave the chicken to marinate for a minimum of 2 hours but preferably overnight. Ensure you remove the chicken from the fridge about an hour before you want to cook it so that it has enough time to warm up to room temperature.

When you are ready to cook, heat the grill to its highest setting and preheat your oven to 180°C/fan 170°C/350°F/gas mark 4.

To prepare your kebabs: take two long metal skewers and lay them parallel to one another – your aim is to build a 'ladder'. Take a chicken thigh and loosely roll it up into a cigar shape with the skinned side facing out. Skewer the chicken thigh with one of the skewers about 1cm to the left of centre. Push the skewer all the way through so that the thigh ends up near the base of the skewer. Push the second skewer through the thigh about 1cm to the right of centre and again thread the thigh all the way to the base of the skewer.

CONTINUED OVERLEAF

Repeat the process with four more thighs, pushing them tightly against one another. Take two more skewers and repeat the process with the remaining chicken thighs.

Lay the kebabs on your grill tray and position on the rung closest to the grill element. Grill the chicken for about 8-10 minutes on each side, by which time the chicken will have browned and even be charred in small patches. Check the chicken is cooked at this point, the only certain way to do this is to cut into the thickest part of the kebab and have a look inside – if there is any pink flesh or juice your kebab needs to go through a hot oven (200°C) for a few minutes. If the juice runs clear and the flesh has turned white your kebab is cooked.

Mix the parsley and mint leaves with the chopped tomatoes and season generously with salt and pepper.

Lay your cooked kebab on to a clean chopping board, and either carve the meat from the skewers on to the board, or alternatively push the meat off the skewers and roughly chop.

Toast your pittas, slice open and stuff with a combination of chopped meat and herb salad. Top with chilli sauce, if using, before greedily gobbling down your delicious homemade kebab.

LAMB DONER KEBAB

SERVES 4

Spiced succulent pieces of grilled lamb meat served in soft pittas
and topped with crunchy salad is similar to the takeaway version
in concept, but completely different in terms of flavour.

**PREP TIME: 15 MINS,
PLUS MARINATING TIME
COOKING TIME: 15 MINS**

1 tbsp ground cumin
3 tbsp olive oil
3 cloves garlic, minced
1kg lamb leg or shoulder
    steaks, chopped into
    3cm chunks
1 large red onion, roughly
    chopped into thin wedges
4 large pitta breads, to serve
½ iceberg lettuce, shredded,
    to serve
salt and freshly ground
    black pepper
chilli sauce, to serve
garlic and onion dip,
    to serve

Spoon the ground cumin in to a bowl along with the
olive oil, garlic and a generous amount of pepper. Mix
the ingredients together until combined. Add the lamb
and red onion. Work the marinade into the meat and
onion, this is easily done with a spoon, but I find getting
your hands in the mix works best.

Leave the meat to marinate for a minimum of 2 hours
but preferably overnight. If marinating overnight, ensure
you remove the meat from the fridge at least 1 hour before
cooking to warm up to room temperature.

When ready to cook, preheat your grill to its highest setting.

Tip the meat and onion on to a tray lined with tin foil, and
pour over any residual marinade. Season the meat
generously with salt at this point, and slide the tray under
the grill as close to the hot element as you are able. Grill for
6–7 minutes on each side, before removing and allowing to
rest for 5 minutes – just enough time to prepare your pittas.

Toast your pittas, cut them open and stuff with the shredded
lettuce. Fill the pittas with the cooked meat, then drizzle
with the chilli sauce and garlic and onion dip. Serve up your
kebabs with not a drunk in sight.

CORNISH PASTIES

The Cornish pasty is steeped in centuries of history that all started down the mines of Cornwall and Devon. Its appeal has survived many variations, so much so that it has been given protected status by the EU. Hopefully my version doesn't contravene international law; one thing is for certain, it makes the perfect snack to be enjoyed hot or cold.

PREP TIME: 30 MINS
COOKING TIME: 35 MINS

plain flour, for dusting
**2 x 500g block shortcrust
   pastry**
**250g rump steak, chopped
   into 5mm pieces**
**250g red potatoes, chopped
   into 5mm pieces**
**150g swede, peeled and
   chopped into 5mm pieces**
**1 small onion, chopped
   into 5mm pieces**
1 egg, beaten, for glazing
**salt and freshly ground
   black pepper**

Preheat your oven to 180°C/fan 170°C/350°F/gas mark 4. Line a baking tray with baking parchment.

Lightly dust a clean surface with flour and roll out your pastry to a thickness of about 5mm. Using a small plate as a template cut out four discs, about 20cm in diameter. This may require you to re-roll the pastry.

Mix the steak, potatoes, swede and onion in a bowl, season with a generous amount of salt and pepper, and give the ingredients a mix.

Make equal piles of the mixture in the centre of each pastry disc, leaving a border of at least 3cm all the way around. Brush the edge of the pastry with a little beaten egg.

Draw two sides up over the filling and press together in the middle over the raw filling. Using your fingers, crimp the joined pastry into the classic pasty shape. This is something that will become easier and more precise with practice.

Transfer the pasties to the prepared baking tray, glaze with more beaten egg and place in the oven for 35–40 minutes, by which time the pastry will have turned a deep golden colour and the filling will be cooked through. To ensure the meat is fully cooked push a sharp knife into the thickest part of a pasty and leave it for 5 seconds. Touch the tip of the knife and if it's hot then the meat is fully cooked.

Let the pasties stand for 5 minutes before digging in. Alternatively these are delicious served at room temperature for a very filling lunch.

BACON and HADDOCK FISH CAKES with PARSLEY SAUCE

SERVES 2 (MAKES 4)

Here the traditional fish cake ingredient – smoked haddock – is mixed with streaky bacon which, when bound with the fluffy mash, adds an extra depth of flavour. Topped with a mellow parsley sauce, the result is a sophisticated dish suited as much to a dinner party as a tasty lunch. Serving one per person along with a portion of wilted spinach works perfectly for lunch, or double up the recipe and serve two per guest for dinner.

PREP TIME: 30 MINS
COOKING TIME: 25 MINS

600ml milk
1 onion, roughly chopped
1 bay leaf
4 rashers of smoked
    streaky bacon
400g smoked haddock,
    undyed if possible, skin on
200g mashed potato (about
    1 large potato, boiled until
    tender then mashed)
6 spring onions, trimmed
    and finely sliced
40g plain flour, plus a little
    extra for dusting
2 eggs
100g fresh breadcrumbs
about 300ml sunflower
    or vegetable oil, for
    shallow-frying
salt and freshly ground
    black pepper
300g baby leaf spinach,
    to serve

For the parsley sauce
40g butter, plus a little
    extra for cooking
1 large bunch of parsley,
    finely chopped
juice of 1 lemon

Pour the milk into a saucepan and add the onion, bay leaf and bacon. Bring the liquid to the boil before sliding in the smoked haddock, placing a lid on your pan and then removing from the heat. Leave the pan like this for about 10 minutes.

Remove the lid and using a slotted spoon, transfer the fish and bacon to a plate. Strain the milk through a sieve and reserve the liquid, discarding the onion and bay leaf. When the fish and bacon are cool enough to handle, strip the skin from the fish and using your fingers break the fish up into large flakes, discarding any bones as you go. Place the flakes into a bowl. Taking one rasher of bacon at a time chop into small strips, discarding any big pieces of fat. Add to the bowl of fish.

Add the mashed potato to the fish and bacon along with the spring onions. Season with a generous amount of salt and pepper before mixing thoroughly. Divide the mixture into four equal amounts, then mould into patty shapes.

Tip some flour on to a plate, and crack the eggs into a bowl and whisk them. Finally tip the breadcrumbs on to a plate. Taking each patty in turn, dust with flour, dip into the egg mix, then roll in breadcrumbs. Place your breadcrumbed

CONTINUED OVERLEAF

fish cakes in the fridge whilst you prepare your parsley sauce.

Melt the butter in a saucepan over a medium-high heat until bubbling. Add the 40g flour and mix in quickly. Cook the butter and flour mixture for about 45 seconds, stirring almost constantly with a wooden spoon. Reduce the heat a little, pour in about a quarter of the strained milk and beat in until totally combined with the flour and butter mix. Pour in another quarter of the milk, and again beat in before pouring in the remainder. Bring the sauce to the boil, stirring regularly. As it heats it will thicken to the consistency of single cream. Add the parsley, lemon juice and a generous amount of salt and pepper. Keep your sauce warm or reheat later.

Heat about 1cm of oil in a high-sided frying pan over a medium–high heat. Remove your fishcakes from the fridge. When the oil is hot enough to crisp a few breadcrumbs quickly it is ready to fry the fishcakes. Carefully slide the fishcakes into the pan. Don't be tempted to cram them all in at once – they need some space. Fry the fishcakes for 2–3 minutes on each side. The fishcakes should turn deliciously dark and golden and the breadcrumbs become crisp. Remove the cooked fish cakes to a piece of clean kitchen paper to drain any excess oil.

Quickly wipe any excess oil from the frying pan and place back over a high heat. When hot add the spinach along with a generous amount of salt and pepper, and fry, stirring regularly for about 1 minute by which time the spinach will have wilted. Serve up your fishcakes on top of a portion of wilted spinach and finish with lashings of warm parsley sauce.

PICKLED EGGS

MAKES 8

These slightly odd beauties are a peculiarity of British culture. Although a bit out of fashion these days, there was a time when pubs and chip shops all over England would have a jar of pickled eggs on their shelves. As you might guess they go very well with beer and fish 'n' chips, as well as being a very good addition to tartare sauce. If you love pickles then have a go at these for something a little different. The eggs will be ready to eat after a day, and if stored in airtight sterilised jars the eggs can pickle for a month in the fridge. The flavour becomes stronger the longer they are left.

PREP TIME: 10 MINS
COOKING TIME: 10 MINS,
PLUS PICKLING TIME

8 eggs, at room temperature
500ml white wine vinegar
1 onion, finely sliced
1 tbsp yellow mustard seeds
1 tbsp coriander seeds

Bring a pan of water to the boil and carefully lower in the eggs. Boil for 10 minutes before removing and running under cold water to cool. When cool enough to handle, peel the eggs and place in the bottom of a sterilised jar (see page 7).

Pour the vinegar and 300ml water into a saucepan and add the onion, mustard seeds and coriander seeds. Bring the liquid to the boil and simmer for 5 minutes until the onion has just softened but is still holding its shape.

Pour the boiling liquid over the cooked eggs, and leave to cool to room temperature. When cool, close the lid and leave in the fridge. The eggs will be ready to eat after one day.

BEEF and ALE PIE

SERVES 6

Beef pie is the edible version of a plump sofa in front of an open fire.
Everything about this meal, even the making of it is comforting; from
the delicious aroma of browning meat to the thick gravy-slicked
mouthfuls, you will feel your soul glowing every step of the way.

PREP TIME: 40 MINS
COOKING TIME: 2 HOURS

vegetable oil, for frying
75g plain flour, plus a little
    extra for dusting
1.5kg stewing beef (I like
    to use shin), chopped
    into 3cm chunks
2 carrots, cut into 1cm dice
4 sticks celery, trimmed
    and cut into 1cm dice
1 large onion, cut into
    1cm dice
1 bay leaf
6cm piece orange peel
1 star anise
2 sprigs of thyme
2 tbsp tomato purée
500ml light ale
250ml beef stock
1 x 320g pre-rolled sheet
    of puff pastry
1 egg, whisked
salt and freshly ground
    black pepper

Heat some oil in a large ovenproof pan over a medium-
high heat.

Whilst the oil is heating up, tip the flour on to a plate and
season well with salt and pepper. Dust the meat with the
75g flour, patting it to shake off any excess. Add enough
chunks of the meat to cover the base of the pan – do not
pile the meat up. It is likely you will have to brown the
meat in batches.

Fry the meat for about 5 minutes, turning a couple of
times until it turns a dark golden brown. Remove the
browned meat to a plate and continue cooking the rest.

When you have browned all the meat add a little more oil
and drop in the carrots, celery and onion. Fry the vegetables
for 5 minutes, stirring regularly, by which time they will
begin to soften. Add the bay leaf, orange peel, star anise
and thyme. Continue to fry for a further 2 minutes,
stirring regularly.

Squeeze in the tomato purée, and immediately stir to
combine with the other ingredients. Continue to fry for
a further 45 seconds, stirring, before pouring in the ale
and beef stock.

Reduce the heat a little. It is important to bring the
mixture to the boil slowly to avoid the ale turning bitter.

CONTINUED OVERLEAF

BEEF AND ALE PIE
CONTINUED

As the liquid comes to the boil, skim off any froth that rises to the top. Tumble the browned chunks of meat back into the liquid and bring the whole lot slowly to the boil. Reduce the heat to a simmer, and cook like this for about 1½ hours, by which time the meat will have become very tender. If it hasn't then continue to cook until it is.

Tip the whole stew into a colander set over a large saucepan. Put the cooked meat and vegetables to one side, picking out the whole herbs, orange peel and star anise, then place the strained liquid back over a high heat, and reduce by a third – it should reach the consistency of single cream.

Tip the meat and vegetables back into the liquid and stir to mix. Tip the whole lot into a 24cm pie dish and leave to cool to room temperature.

Preheat your oven to 190°C/fan 180°C/375°F/gas mark 5.

Lightly dust a clean surface with a little flour. Unroll your pastry on to the floured surface, and I always like to give it a little extra roll just to make sure it is just less than 5mm thick.

Using your finger or a brush, moisten the edge of your pie dish with the egg. Use a sharp knife to cut a couple of long pastry strips about 1cm thick, they don't have to be perfect. Push the strips on to the edge of the dish, these will help the pastry lid stick to the dish.

Position your pastry over the top of the filling, and push down all the way around the edge to seal, give it a little crimp if you like, or just use a fork to push down and give a simple pattern. Trim the excess pastry around the dish, brush the top with beaten egg and place in the oven.

Bake your pie for about 35 minutes by which time the filling will be piping hot and the puff pastry risen and a very satisfying, rich golden brown. Serve to family and friends and enjoy the silence.

NEW WAVE MUSHY PEAS

SERVES 4

Because the classic marrowfat mushy peas in tins are so readily available on supermarket shelves I have decided instead to create a different recipe that is fresher, lighter and ultimately very different to its predecessor. I, like many others, am a fan of classic mushy peas which are essentially soaked and boiled marrowfat peas, but if you are looking for something different and arguably more versatile then look no further than this recipe.

PREP TIME: 10 MINS
COOKING TIME: 10 MINS

small knob of butter
1 shallot, finely diced
1 red chilli, deseeded
   and finely diced
450g frozen peas or
   petit pois
½ bunch of mint, leaves
   only, finely sliced
2 tsp fish sauce
salt and freshly ground
   black pepper

Bring a pot of water to the boil. Meanwhile, melt the knob of butter in a medium saucepan over a medium-high heat. When the butter has melted and is lightly bubbling add the shallot and chilli. Fry for about 2 minutes.

When the water is boiling drop in the peas and cook for about 1 minute at which point they should be warmed through and vibrant green in colour. Quickly drain the peas through a sieve and immediately add to the frying shallot and chilli.

Toss the ingredients together, then remove from the heat and use a potato masher to lightly crush the peas. I like a roughly mashed consistency that still has a few whole peas.

When you are happy with the consistency add the mint leaves, fish sauce and a generous pinch of salt and pepper. Mix one last time to combine all the ingredients, then serve up alongside almost any piece of roasted or fried fish or meat for something a little different.

CHAPTER
EIGHT *

SWEET

* THINGS

Every meal should have a sweet finale and even though desserts in takeaway restaurants are often ignored or treated as an afterthought, this chapter is anything but. The recipes here don't necessarily come from takeaway menus but I hope they might tap into that part of the brain which craves the homely taste of takeaway food – the bit that likes a little old-school luxury wrapped up in Mum's cooking. And let's face it, even though we may not order our dessert from the takeaway menu, how many of us open the cupboard to reach for a chocolate bar or nip to the corner shop for a packet of doughnuts for a sweet fix after dinner...

The recipes here also come with a diverse range of flavours from both East and West, so there's something for everyone.

BLUEBERRY *and* WHITE CHOCOLATE CHEESECAKE

SERVES 6-8

This is one of the most seductive flavour combinations that exists. The slightly tart blueberries tame the sweetness of the white chocolate and both flavours combine perfectly with the slightly sour tones of cream cheese.

PREP TIME: 25 MINS
COOKING TIME: 5 MINS,
PLUS 4 HOURS' SETTING TIME

200g digestive biscuits
90g unsalted butter, melted
sunflower or vegetable
  oil, for greasing
200g blueberries, plus
  extra for decorating
200g white chocolate,
  broken into small pieces,
  plus extra for grating
125g cream cheese
125g crème fraîche
3 egg whites
90g caster sugar

Place the biscuits in a food processor and blitz them until they have the texture of breadcrumbs. With the processor blade still turning add the melted butter and continue running the machine for 30 seconds to make sure the two ingredients are well mixed together. If you don't have a food processor then place the biscuits in a sealed bag and bash away at them with a rolling pin, then mix with the butter.

Oil the base of a 25cm loose-bottomed tart tin. Tip the biscuit crumbs into the tin and flatten the surface with back of a spoon. Tumble the blueberries on to the base, distributing them as evenly as possible. Place the tart case in the fridge whilst you continue.

Place the chocolate in a heatproof bowl resting over a saucepan of simmering water. Make sure the base of the bowl doesn't come into contact with the water as it will split the chocolate. Leave the chocolate to melt for 5 minutes, before removing the bowl from above the pan and leaving to cool a little.

Place the cream cheese and crème fraîche in a large bowl and beat with a wooden spoon until they are completely combined.

In another bowl whisk the egg whites using an electric whisk if you have one, or elbow grease if you don't. Whisk the whites until they thicken and turn frothy, having at

CONTINUED OVERLEAF

least doubled in volume. Add a quarter of the sugar and whisk again for 1 minute to fully incorporate the sugar before adding a further quarter and whisking again for 1 minute. Continue the process until all the sugar has been used and the egg whites have become thick and glossy.

Scape the melted white chocolate into the cream cheese mixture and immediately beat together with a wooden spoon. When you are happy the ingredients are fully blended, dollop in roughly a third of the whisked egg white mix and beat into the other ingredients. Carefully dollop the remaining two thirds of whisked white into the bowl and using a metal spoon and a gentle folding and stirring action, work the whites into the other ingredients to preserve as much of the air as possible.

Remove the tart case from the fridge, and if necessary redistribute the blueberries. Gently drop the velvety mixture on top of the blueberries and biscuits. Even out the surface, pushing the white chocolate mixture all the way to the edges with a spoon. Grate the extra white chocolate over the top and decorate with blueberries. Place the cheesecake back in the fridge and leave to set for at least 4 hours.

When the time comes, gently tease the cheesecake from its case and serve huge wedges accompanied by nothing but a huge grin.

APPLE *and* SULTANA SAMOSAS

MAKES 6

Apples and sultanas spiced with a sprinkling of cinnamon, all wrapped up in a neat filo parcel and baked till crisp; these little parcels of joy are an indulgent climax to any meal. Once cooked and cooled this dessert freezes very well and can be reheated straight from frozen in a hot oven.

PREP TIME: 40 MINS
COOKING TIME: 35 MINS

70g sultanas
knob of unsalted butter,
    plus extra melted
    butter for brushing
3cm piece fresh ginger,
    minced
2 large Bramley apples,
    peeled, cored and
    roughly chopped
    into 2cm pieces
50g caster sugar
1 tsp ground cinnamon
1 x 270g pack filo pastry
2 tbsp chopped hazelnuts
icing sugar, to serve
shop-bought custard,
    to serve

Preheat your oven to 180°C/fan 170°C/350°F/gas mark 4.

Tip the sultanas into a bowl and cover with warm water. Leave the sultanas to plump up for about 10 minutes before draining.

Heat the butter in a medium saucepan over a medium-high heat. When the butter is lightly bubbling, add the ginger and fry, stirring almost constantly, for 20 seconds. Next, add the apples, caster sugar and cinnamon. Toss the ingredients together and cook for about 3 minutes. You want the apple to just about still be holding its shape but be almost completely soft. Tumble in the soaked sultanas, stir to incorporate and then leave your apple mixture to one side to cool a little.

Remove the pastry from its packaging, unravel three sheets and place the remaining sheets under a damp tea towel so they don't dry out. Lay one sheet of the filo in front of you on a chopping board, and liberally brush it with some melted butter. Lay the second sheet on top and again brush with melted butter before topping with the final sheet.

Cut the pastry into thirds lenghtways to create three pastry strips that should be roughly 15cm wide and 25cm long.

Working with one strip at a time, dollop a quarter of the apple mixture at the top short end of the pastry, ensuring

CONTINUED OVERLEAF

APPLE AND
SULTANA SAMOSAS
CONTINUED

a generous 3cm border all the way around. Pick up the top corner of the pastry and fold it straight over the filling until it reaches the opposite edge. Next fold the triangle over itself to enclose another side. Continue folding the pastry in consecutive triangles until all of the edges are closed and you have run out of pastry to fold.

Ensure the samosa is sealed all over. Place the samosa on to a flat baking tray and repeat the process with the remaining pastry and apple mixture. Sprinkle the samosas with the chopped hazelnuts.

Place the tray in the oven and bake for about 30 minutes, by which time the pastry will have turned crisp and invitingly golden. Remove from the oven, dust with icing sugar and serve on top of a pool of cold custard. Yum.

ALMOND *and* CARDAMOM CHILLED RICE PUDDING

SERVES 4

This is a rice pudding like no other you have tried. By using rice flour instead of rice grains the resulting dessert becomes a smooth and delicate end to your meal rather than the admittedly delicious, but more heavy classic pudding your gran may have whipped up for you. I've opted for almond milk and cardamom to add an Indian twist.

PREP TIME: 20 MINS
COOKING TIME: 10 MINS,
PLUS 3 HOURS' COOLING

1 vanilla pod or 1 tbsp
vanilla extract if
you can't find pods
500ml almond milk
150ml double cream
6 cardamom pods,
lightly crushed with
palm of your hand
75g caster sugar
40g rice flour
pomegranate seeds,
to serve
shelled pistachio nuts,
roughly chopped,
to serve

Using a small knife cut the vanilla pod down its length. Use the point of your knife to scrape the seeds from the inside.

Pour the almond milk and double cream into a saucepan and add the scraped vanilla seeds along with the cardamom pods. Bring the mixture to the boil over a medium-high heat, stirring regularly to avoid burning the milk. When the milk has come to the boil, remove the mixture from the heat and leave to infuse for 30 minutes before straining through a sieve into a bowl or jug. Mix in the caster sugar.

Tip the rice flour into a clean saucepan and place over a medium-high heat. Cook the flour for 1 minute, stirring almost constantly. Take the pan off the heat and pour in roughly a quarter of the infused milk. Beat the ingredients together with a wooden spoon until they are fully combined.

Add another quarter of the milk and place the pan back over a medium-high heat. Once incorporated, pour in the remaining milk, and bring the whole lot slowly to the boil whilst stirring almost constantly. Let the mix simmer for 30 seconds before removing from the heat and leaving to cool to room temperature.

When the rice pudding mix has cooled divide equally between 4 ramekins or glasses and place in the fridge to cool for a minimum of 2 hours but preferably overnight.

When ready to serve remove the puddings from the fridge and top with pomegranate seeds and chopped pistachios.

MISSISSIPPI MUD PIE

SERVES 6

There is little explanation out there as to why this cake is so called. Maybe it's that the gooey consistency of the cake resembles the muddy banks of the Mississippi. Whatever the reason, my understanding of Mississippi mud pie is a cake that contains as much chocolate as is physically possible. I've controversially opted for a chocolate mousse version, which I think is just a tad lighter and a little more civilised.

PREP TIME: 40 MINS
COOKING TIME: 5 MINS,
PLUS 2 HOURS' COOLING

1 x 230g packet of double chocolate digestive biscuits
80g unsalted butter, melted
250g dark chocolate, broken up into small pieces, plus 50g extra, to decorate
150ml double cream
4 eggs, separated
60g caster sugar
50g white chocolate, to decorate
300g raspberries, to decorate

Place the biscuits in a food processor and blitz to a breadcrumb consistency. If you don't have a food processor then put the biscuits in a sealable plastic bag and use a rolling pin to break up the biscuits. Mix the butter with the crushed biscuits, then tip the mixture into the base of a 20cm springform cake tin. Using the back of a spoon smooth the surface of the biscuits, pushing the buttered crumbs up the side as well to create a bit of a wall. Place the tin in the fridge to help set the base.

Place the broken chocolate in a large, heatproof bowl along with the cream. Sit the bowl over a saucepan of simmering water, ensuring the base of the bowl does not touch the water. Leave the chocolate to melt for 8–10 minutes without disturbing.

Place the egg whites in a large bowl and using an electric hand whisk, beat them for about 1 minute until the whites have more than quadrupled in volume and have become light and fluffy. Tip in the sugar and again beat with the electric whisk. Whisk for about 2 minutes by which time the mixture will have turned glossy and slightly stiff.

Remove the bowl of melted chocolate from the water and gently stir to blend the cream and chocolate together. Let the chocolate cool for 2 minutes before beating in the egg yolks one at a time with a wooden spoon.

Dollop a third of the whisked egg whites into the dark chocolate mix and use a spoon to beat the two mixtures together. Spoon the remaining egg whites into the mix and, using a light circular chopping action, incorporate the egg whites into the dark chocolate mixture, safeguarding as much of the air as possible.

Remove the biscuit base from the fridge and splodge the chocolate mousse mixture into the base. Lightly spread it around to make an even layer. Smooth the top of the mousse using a spoon that has been warmed under the hot tap for a few seconds. Place the tin back in the fridge and chill for a minimum of 2 hours; preferably overnight.

When ready to serve, melt the extra dark chocolate and the white chocolate using bowls set over hot water, as described opposite. Decorate the top of the pie with the raspberries, then zig-zag the melted chocolates over the top to give it an awesome finish.

HAZELNUT TIRAMISU

SERVES 8

The joy of a tiramisu is the sponge fingers that are soaked in coffee and slowly soften over time – they give it its unique texture. Instead of just going down the classic route, which mixes sweet Marsala wine or amaretto with the cream cheese, I've plumped for Frangelico – a hazelnut liqueur – which spikes the dish with a distinctively different flavour. I can assure you, you will find it irresistible.

PREP TIME: 30 MINS
COOKING TIME: 0 MINS,
BUT AT LEAST 2 HOURS
TO SET

1 egg, separated
75g caster sugar
500g mascarpone
10 tbsp Frangelico or
    similar hazelnut liqueur
500ml cold strong coffee
    (I use a cafetière)
350g sponge fingers
    (just under 50)
100g hazelnuts,
    toasted and chopped
30g dark chocolate,
    to decorate

Put the egg yolk and sugar into a bowl and whisk until the yolk pales in colour and the sugar is completely worked in. In a separate bowl, whisk the egg white until it has more than doubled in volume and has become thick with air.

Add the mascarpone and 3 tablespoons of the Frangelico to the beaten egg yolk and beat together with a wooden spoon until the ingredients are fully blended. Beat a third of the whisked egg whites into the marscarpone mixture before gently folding through the remaining two thirds, trying to keep as much air in the mixture as possible. Place this mix in the fridge until ready to use.

Pour the coffee into a large flat tray, add the remaining Frangelico and mix well. Take a few sponge fingers at a time and drop them in to the liquid, turning a couple of times. Swiftly pluck them from the coffee and start to line them up in the base of a 20cm square dish. Continue until you have used roughly half the sponge fingers and have covered the base of the dish.

Remove the mascarpone mixture from the fridge and dollop roughly half of it on top of the soaked biscuits. Smooth the surface using the back of a spoon. Make another layer with the remaining sponge fingers, dipping them then lining them up on top of the mascarpone mixture. Finish with the remaining mascarpone. Place your tiramisu in the fridge and leave to chill for a minimum of 2 hours.

Just before serving scatter the toasted chopped hazelnuts on top and decorate with a generous grating of dark chocolate.

MANGO *and* COCONUT ICE LOLLIES

MAKES 6

When the sun shines and the weather is hot there are few more enjoyable ways to cool down than to devour an ice lolly. You will need to buy some lolly moulds for this recipe but consider them an investment because when you've tried them you are sure to make these lollies again and again...

PREP TIME: 10 MINS
COOKING TIME: 0 MINS, BUT 4 HOURS' FREEZING TIME NEEDED

1 mango, peeled and stoned
200g natural yoghurt
200ml coconut milk
3 tbsp caster sugar
grated zest of 1 lime, plus extra to decorate
2 tbsp desiccated coconut, to decorate

Place the mango flesh in a small food processor and blitz until smooth. If you don't have a food processor then just chop the flesh over and over until you are left with what could be described as mango mince.

Place your puréed mango in a bowl and mix in the yoghurt, coconut milk, sugar and lime zest. Give the ingredients a good mix with a whisk to ensure the sugar is well incorporated and evenly spread.

Pour the mixture into six lolly moulds and place in the freezer. Leave the lollies to freeze for a minimum of 4 hours.

To remove the lollies from their moulds just dunk the moulds into hot water and leave for about 10 seconds, this should loosen the lollies enough for you to pull them out.

DOUGHNUTS

SERVES 4 LUCKY PEOPLE

Yum, yum, yum. Homemade doughnuts served with custard
and jam. These are so easy and so deliciously effective that they
could soon become your signature dinner party dessert.

**PREP TIME: 20 MINS, PLUS
1½ HOURS' PROVING TIME
COOKING TIME: 12–15 MINS**

**300ml milk, warmed
1 x 7g sachet fast-action
    yeast
1 egg
25g unsalted butter
25g caster sugar, plus
    extra for rolling
500g strong white bread
    flour, plus a little extra
    for rolling
6g (roughly 1tsp) fine salt
about 1 litre sunflower
    or vegetable oil, for
    deep-frying, plus a little
    extra for the bowl
shop-bought custard,
    to serve
strawberry or raspberry
    jam, to serve**

Place the warm milk in a bowl and add the yeast. Crack in
the egg and whisk to mix in. Add the butter and caster sugar.
Mix the ingredients together thoroughly with a fork or
whisk until the sugar and yeast have completely dissolved
into the milk. Leave the mixture to stand for 2 minutes.

Tip the flour and salt into a bowl and stir to combine.
Pour the yeast mixture in and start to bring the ingredients
together with a fork. When it becomes hard to mix any more,
tip the batter on to a lightly floured surface and start to
knead with your hands. The dough will come together after
a couple of minutes. Continue to knead the dough for 5
minutes to ensure all the ingredients are well combined.
Work the dough into a neat ball.

Lightly oil a large bowl and place the dough ball in the base.
Cover the dough with cling film and place in a warm place
to rise for 1 hour.

Remove the cling film and tip the dough out on to a newly
floured work surface. Knock the air out of the dough by
kneading it for a couple of minutes.

Line a baking tray with some greaseproof paper and scatter
a little flour over the paper. Divide the dough into 13 equal
pieces, roughly 70g each, and roll each piece into a small
ball, placing the balls on to the floured paper as you go.
Leave the balls, uncovered, to rise for a further 15 minutes.

Heat about 15cm of the oil in a deep saucepan to 170°C and
scatter some caster sugar over a flat baking tray or plate.

If you don't have a thermometer then you can tell when the oil is at 170°C by dropping a cube of bread into it; the bread should be golden brown in about 40 seconds.

Carefully lower the dough balls into the hot oil but do not overcrowd the pan as the balls will expand whilst cooking. Cook in batches if you have to. Fry the doughnuts for 3 minutes before flipping them over and frying for a further 3 minutes.

Remove the cooked doughnuts to a clean piece of kitchen paper to remove excess oil before rolling quickly in the caster sugar. Serve your warm doughnuts with custard and jam.

BLACK FOREST GATEAU

SERVES 8

One of the poster boys of 1980s food, this cake has had a bit of a resurgence – and so it should. It is a perfect combination of chocolate and cherries all whipped up in a cacophony of cream and sponge. I've taken a great shortcut in this recipe using cherry cordial which is widely available in supermarkets, and have given my cake its very own tribute to the 1980s with a dressing of toasted coconut.

PREP TIME: 45 MINS
COOKING TIME: 35 MINS

400ml cherry cordial
1 star anise
2 tsp vanilla extract
175g softened unsalted butter, plus extra for greasing
250g caster sugar
3 eggs
150ml sunflower oil
150ml soured cream
90g cocoa powder, plus a little extra for dusting
250g self-raising flour
200g dark chocolate
450ml double cream, whipped, plus a little extra for decorating
2 tbsp icing sugar
150g desiccated coconut, toasted
12 cherries

Pour the cherry cordial into a saucepan and add the star anise. Bring the liquid to the boil, then reduce the heat. Simmer for 5 minutes, by which time the cordial will have reduced and taken on the flavour of the star anise. Leave this mixture to cool and when cold, remove the star anise and discard, then stir in the vanilla extract.

Preheat your oven to 180°C/fan 170°C/350°F/gas mark 4. Butter two 20cm cake tins.

Place the caster sugar and butter in a large mixing bowl and use a wooden spoon to beat them together until creamy and pale. Crack the eggs in one by one and use a whisk to mix them with the creamed sugar and butter. Mix the oil and soured cream and add to the mixture, again using a whisk to combine with the other ingredients.

Tip the cocoa powder and self-raising flour into a bowl and roughly mix with a fork. Add the dry mixture to the bowl of wet ingredients and use a wooden spoon to bring everything together into a cake mix. Divide the mixture between the prepared cake tins. Place the tins in the oven and bake for 25–30 minutes. The cake is cooked when a knife or skewer inserted into the centre reappears clean. When you are happy that the cakes are cooked, remove them from the oven and place the tins on a wire rack until cool enough

CONTINUED OVERLEAF

to handle. Remove the cakes from the tins and place back on the wire rack to cool completely.

Place the chocolate and 250ml of the double cream in a large bowl resting over a saucepan of boiling water. Don't let the base of the bowl come into contact with the boiling water, otherwise it will split the chocolate. Leave the chocolate to melt into the double cream for about 10 minutes, giving it a stir halfway through. When you are happy that the chocolate has almost all melted take the bowl off the heat and mix the ingredients together with a wooden spoon, this should create a lovely chocolate ganache icing. Leave to one side.

When the cakes have completely cooled use a bread knife to carefully and evenly slice each one in half across the diameter to give you 4 thin cakes.

Whip the remaining cream with the icing sugar.

Place one of your cakes on to a cake plate or serving platter and drizzle over a quarter of the cherry cordial, letting each spoonful be absorbed by the sponge before adding the next and ensuring you drizzle all the way to the edges. Spoon a third of the remaining double cream on top and spread all over. Top with another layer of sponge and again spoon over a quarter of the cordial mixture and a layer of double cream. Repeat this process until you have a 4-tier cake.

Spoon the chocolate icing on top of the cake and let it drizzle over the edges. Use a palette knife or butter knife to smooth the icing evenly all over. Press the toasted coconut on to the sides of the cake.

Dust your cake with cocoa powder, then pipe or spoon 12 mounds of whipped cream around the top edge of the cake and top each one with a cherry. Stand back and admire your retro creation.

STICKY TOFFEE PUDDING

SERVES 6

One of the most iconic British desserts, this pudding deserves its worldwide renown. Contrary to the name there isn't any toffee in the pudding, instead the sticky toffee-esque consistency and sharp sweetness are provided by dates and black treacle.

PREP TIME: 20 MINS
COOKING TIME: 45–50 MINS

240g softened unsalted butter, cubed, plus extra for greasing
325g pitted dates, roughly chopped into small pieces
2 tbsp black treacle
360g demerara sugar
250g self-raising flour
1½ tsp bicarbonate of soda
3 eggs
150ml milk
2 tsp vanilla extract
450ml double cream

Preheat your oven to 160°C/150°C fan/325°F/gas mark 3. Butter and line a 23cm springform cake tin with baking parchment.

Place the dates in a heatproof bowl and pour over 250ml boiling water. Dip a metal tablespoon into the hot water and use it to spoon the black treacle into the soaking date mix. Give the ingredients a brief stir and allow to sit for 20 minutes.

Meanwhile, place 210g of the demerara sugar and half the butter in a large bowl and use a wooden spoon to beat them until the butter turns a pale yellow colour. This can also be done with an electric hand whisk if you have one.

In a separate bowl mix the flour and bicarbonate of soda. Spoon a couple of tablespoons of the flour mixture into the creamed butter and sugar – this will help prevent the mixture from splitting.

Crack the eggs into a bowl and add the milk and vanilla extract. Briefly whisk the ingredients together. Pour half this liquid into the creamed butter and sugar mixture and using a combination of wooden spoon and whisk, work the mixtures together. Pour in the remaining milk mix and work in.

Add the soaked dates along with all of their soaking water and give the whole lot a good stir to combine the ingredients

CONTINUED OVERLEAF

thoroughly. Finally add the remaining flour and beat the whole lot together until you have a loose cake batter.

Pour the mix into the prepared tin and place in the oven. Bake for 45–50 minutes, covering with foil if the top looks as though it's colouring too much. You can tell when your cake is cooked by inserting a skewer or small knife into the centre; if the knife emerges clean your cake is cooked.

Whilst the cake is baking tip the remaining butter and demerara sugar into a saucepan along with the double cream. Bring the ingredients to the boil over a medium-high heat stirring regularly. Simmer the ingredients for 30 seconds before removing from the heat.

When it's ready, take the cake out the oven and let it sit for at least 15 minutes before removing it from the cake tin. Serve hot or cold smothered in the toffee sauce. Dried fruit has never tasted so good.

BREAD *and* BUTTER PUDDING

SERVES 6

What is at its heart a very humble and unassuming pudding has been tampered with to the point that many recipes now involve chocolate, dates, whisky and hot cross buns. I think all these variations just divert from the beautiful simplicity of the original, so I will not mess about with added extravagance and simply pass on a recipe that was given to me by a very dear old friend.

PREP TIME: 25 MINS
COOKING TIME: 35 MINS

150g softened unsalted
   butter, plus extra
   for greasing
50ml dark rum
150g sultanas
1 loaf of thick-sliced white
   bread, crusts removed
6 eggs, 3 of them separated
450ml double cream,
   plus extra to serve
1 vanilla pod, split in
   half and seeds scraped
90g caster sugar
3 tbsp demerara sugar

Preheat your oven to 170°C/160°C fan/340°F/gas mark 3½. Butter the inside of a 28 x 15cm baking dish.

Heat the rum either in the microwave or over a low heat in a saucepan. When warm, remove from the heat, add the sultanas and leave to plump up.

Butter the bread on one side, then cut the slices into triangles. Arrange your triangles of bread evenly in the baking dish, butter-side up, overlapping as you go. Drain the sultanas, keeping the rum, and scatter them over the bread slices, ensuring that some
drop into the gaps between the triangles.

Whisk together 3 egg yolks and 3 whole eggs. Add the leftover rum, the double cream, vanilla seeds and caster sugar. Whisk until all of the ingredients are well combined. Pour this raw-custard mix over the arranged bread triangles. The bread should ultimately absorb all of the mixture but it might be necessary to pour some custard, wait for it to be absorbed, and then pour more.

Let the pudding sit for about 10 minutes before scattering the top with the demerara sugar and placing in the oven.

Bake the pudding for 35 minutes by which time the tips of the bread will have browned and the custard just set. Serve huge mounds of pudding drenched in extra cream.

INDEX

ACKNOWLEDGEMENTS

★
_____

Thank you to those at Orion: Amanda for taking the punt, Kate for constant, relaxed support and Helen for helping with the look of the book.

To those on the photo shoot: Kris, not only for controlling the shutter, but also for tireless energy in search of perfection – I appreciate every minute you spent with the photos. Faith, for your all-round can-do attitude, and good coffee. Alex and Emma for control, vision and appetite. Leonie, for keeping me in check and cooking excellence. To Jenny for the beautiful plates and props.

Imogen (and Kate again) for bringing order to my words whilst not haranguing me for my lax attitude towards deadlines.

To every home economist and chef I have worked with over the last decade you have been so generous with your knowledge and skills; I have been nothing other than privileged to have learned from you all.

To my friends for laughter.

To my family: Mum, your food will always be my favourite. Without knowing it you set me on this course with kimchi, rice and fish stews. Dad and Rich you have always been there, without you all I would have nothing.

… And finally to Han, Theo and Tallulah; my world.